T0067157

Volume 1: Turnkey Projects

RISK AND EXPOSURE IN SOFTWARE *and* IT PROJECTS

Deep Legal Insights

Farouq Alhefnawi

authorHOUSE®

AuthorHouse™ UK
1663 Liberty Drive
Bloomington, IN 47403 USA
www.authorhouse.co.uk
Phone: 0800.197.4150

Published by AuthorHouse 02/10/2015

ISBN: 978-1-4969-9968-9 (sc)
ISBN: 978-1-4969-9529-2 (hc)
ISBN: 978-1-4969-9969-6 (e)

Print information available on the last page.

This book is printed on acid-free paper.

Dedication

With a firm notion, I believe that legal knowledge is at its best when utilized to help people (in any discipline) to avoid legal caveats and perils thrown in their way. This study is a sincere endeavour to apply the same notion in a small rocky corner of our life, aiming to assist IT professionals everywhere, particularly in ME, to overcome such caveats and perils. That is because when someone bases his behaviour on principals, the majority of his decisions are already made.

Acknowledgment

From the core of my heart, I am grateful to:

- My wife; Nagda, who has departed our world just before sending this book to printing. Nagda has left a legacy of love, loyalty, support, endless fidelity and noble values. She will be always remembered for the meaning she brought to my life, the life of my small family and to our community. Nagda will remain for me the singular source of inspiration, wisdom and love.
- Marwa, Mohamed, and Nour (my small family), your unmatchable love and sincerity, your belief in me enabled me immensely to bring many of my dreams into reality, including this work.
- Ms. Dina Badereldin (legal counsel). Dina! You have enriched this book with strenuous efforts and sincere support. You have done extensive Internet research and in depth navigation on the Middle Eastern (ME) legal system and other jurisdictions. Thank you, Dina, for your sincere voluntary efforts.
- Mrs. Leilani (personal assistant). You have come up with great and dynamic assistance in the entire process of reviewing, editing, and formatting this book.
- Ms Nudrat Siddiqui (proof-reader). Thanks, Nudrat, for always being there in the form of your heartfelt efforts. You have embellished this book with your creative touch with words.
- The ME legal team of Huawei Technologies. Special thanks to UAE team, Nida, Monqez, and Renyangtuo, for their valuable thoughts and for enjoying together the spirit of teamwork and facing the daily stress with a smiling attitude.

This Book

It is quite clear – as depicted by various studies and scientific statistics and indeed, from personal experience – that there exists a high degree of risk in the execution of software and IT projects, owing to, among other reasons the recent history of this realm; coupled with its unique nature of ***"invisibility and intangibility".*** This is true since both parties enter into an agreement over the implementation of intangible products, unlike the case with other industries offering tangible products, and as a result a high degree of ***uncertainty and unpredictably*** exists in the software industry. Neither party shall be able to see the final products until they are completed. Moreover, they will not experience their actual performance until they are loaded into live environment operation. This is when the problems and risks associated with the products and systems become apparent; that is assuming the project is completed and not prematurely terminated.

Whatever the cause for project failure, what is definite is that contracts and contracting processes pertaining to software and IT projects can play a significant role in assisting both parties in successfully and safely concluding the project. I adamantly believe that contracts signed between parties engaged in software and IT projects, are one of the most effective tools for alleviating the perils and caveats persistent within this important industry. It indeed can contribute significantly in the success of such projects; which make contracts an essentially crucial aspect that is more often than not overlooked by many researchers, stakeholders and professionals.

From here emanated the notion of this book of closely examining this phenomenon, but from a legal approach and specifically from a contractual perspective; i.e. how can a ***"coherent and fair"*** contract play a significant role in mitigating risks and exposure in software and IT projects.

Farouq
October 2014

Book Structure

The law for contract (and the laws in general) do not exist in a vacuum, but are influenced with the overall environment in which these laws apply. The legal principles play a fundamental role in all aspects of our lives and indeed in the business practices. With that said, this book has focused on the great interrelation between Law and Business; that is between the legal principles and the actual business practices in the software and IT industry and more particularly in IT projects. In addition to giving a cavernous analysis, it is also meticulously focused on the role which can be played by such principles in the success of IT projects. On this basis, the book has been structured to bring into focus the necessity of understanding the business and legal environment in which the software and IT projects exist, the role of contracts and the role of the in-house legal counsel in the success of such projects.

Based on the above, the first four chapters pivoted on setting a scene, by giving an entire background of the legal and business environment surrounding the software and IT projects, including a general overview of the software and IT industry, the different types of potential pitfalls involved in its projects, along with a comprehensive background of the software and IT contracts. Chapter three, provides an extensive analysis to the legal principles governing the contractual process for software and IT projects in one of the legal jurisdictions in which the author has dexterity.

After sketching the initial scene, chapter 5 is intended to scrupulously examine the main concept of the book, and to interrelate a fascinating combination between business background and the complicated legal principles; o see how it works in the real world. In this regard, we have chosen one of the most famous types of projects in the software and IT industry i.e. "turnkey projects", to apply such concepts and principles on a real transaction by analyzing the turnkey transaction, combine the business background with the legal concepts and principles, and show how together they help to keep the embedded risk in IT projects at bay.

Chapter 6 of the book comprises the denouements, key insights of the premise on which the book was drafted, along with a practical guidance that can lend a hand to the contracting parties in reducing the associated risks in IT projects or avoiding them altogether. Since we strongly believe in the overall role played by the in-house counsels in IT organizations, the last chapter was dedicated to provide the legal counsels in IT companies with specific guidance on how to deal with software and IT projects and participate effectively in the success of such projects.

It is worthy to note that the ME legal system has been used as a specimen jurisdiction where the legal principles and the contract have been analyzed and anatomized in a simplified and practical manner. Nevertheless, the ideas, advices and insights presented in this book, are applicable to any other jurisdiction, just by making some necessary adjustments to the specifics and particulars of that jurisdiction. Hence, the concepts can indeed help the IT professionals universally.

It is also important to note that software and IT projects referred to in this book are projects that, to a great extent, fall within the "turnkey projects" category. Accordingly, when we talk about the high rate of failure in IT projects, we mainly mean the high rate of failure in turnkey projects. Risk and exposure in other types of projects such as IT outsourcing, license, software development, and others will be discussed in volume two of this book.

Contents

Chapter 3: Legal Environment

Chapter 4: Software and IT Contracts

Chapter 5: Contracting for Turnkey Projects

Chapter 6: Denouements and Key Insights

List of Figures

Chapter 3

Chapter 4

Chapter 5

List of Tables

Chapter 2

Chapter 4

Chapter 5

Chapter 1
IT INDUSTRY; OVERVIEW

Aim of the Chapter

This chapter aims mainly to set the scene and shed dim but focused light on the software industry in a general sense and on the potential risks involved in its projects; their success rates; and reasons for failure. The chapter also aims to substantiate that a contractual system, being a preventive strategy against the occurrence of complications, can play a significant role in increasing the success rates and reducing the probabilities for the failure of IT projects.

Background

There exists no definitive definitions for the software and Information Technology (IT) industry; however, we may consider the following realms of computers, software, and IT:

Hardware – Software is loaded on these tangible entities. The most prominent hardware manufacturers worldwide are many, such as HP, Dell, Cisco, and Huawei.

Software – These are the astounding logical entities invented in the middle of last century, which have baffled legal experts, in terms of their legal adaptation and the means to supplement legal sanctuary over them. From a technical perspective, software comprises a bundle of instructions that are loaded onto a computer machine. It designates the operations and implements the series of instructions according to a specific sequence.

These instructions are either stored in the computer's memory or on tangible storage medium, whereby the computer machine is able to read and achieve pre-set specific functions by means of data processing. Software, in this sense, includes operating systems (or systems software) in addition to application software. The primeval version of software is written in a language that is readable by humans (termed source code), together with a version that is readable only by a machine (referred to as an object code).[1]

Systems – Intermittently referred to as "solutions", these information systems emanate from the integration among the hardware, software, and related services. They are considered as an integrated system and not individually. These integrated systems are among the paramount outcomes attained by the software industry, and are comprised of intricate systems and solutions that perform specific functions in all industries. Their design and installation require diverse expertise. The

---

1 See more details on the legal protection of software in my book (in Arabic) *Law of Software*, 77.

implementation of IT systems is one of the most complicated and risky process in IT industry, which this book is focusing on.

Services – Incorporate a set of activities and services that revolve around software and hardware. They encompass particular design, development, installation, customization, testing, and integration activities for systems and information solutions. Other activities also exist within the realm of services, such as software development, software support, publication, and other related services that include training, documentation, consulting, new activities such as IT outsourcing, SaaS (software as a service), software escrow, and many others.

Software and Information Technology

Information Technology – A term that emerged in the 70's to express the convergence of the two grand industries, the computer industry and communications.[2] A fascinating industry materialized from such a convergence, which has infiltrated almost all aspects of life, paving the way for a new world, a new civilization, a new age – that is, the Information Age. This new technology was recognized as Information Technology (IT).

However, for the new industry being associated with numerous expressions– most of which either arduous to define or left to be undefined – we would like to point out some observations for clarification, without delving into excessively technical terms, which are as follows:

- There exist no concrete definitions for the many terms and expressions present in the world of computers, information systems, or information technology, or the digital world that has evolved from them. Quite often, the terms and expressions are utilized interchangeably. For instance, one of the writers[3] cites the law issued in England in 1990 under the title Computer

2 Chris Edward, Nigel Savage, and Ian Walding, *Information Technology & the Law, (1990)* 2nd Edition, page 1

3 Ian J Liod, Information Technology Law, Forth Edition, Oxford Universty Press, page 3.

Misuse, which mentioned the term computer forty-one times, software twenty-nine times, and data twenty-five times. Still, none of these terms was genuinely defined. Similarly, an overwhelming conviction exists that Internet and web are two equivalent terms, even though they are actually not. With the number and exchangeability of terms and expressions involved, we discover that computer, being the foundation of every advancement and the epicentre of all technologies, takes centre stage in the midst of these momentous breakthroughs. At the core, still we find software and IT, which embody the practical and commercial applications of all these technologies.

- Software commands a central position when it comes to all momentous developments and advancements in the realm of computers and information systems. In fact, some writers hold the view that software, being intellectual property bulwarked by law as all others, has commenced to take superiority over any other form of intellectual material, especially in light of the digital age in which we live. It is now possible to develop computer programs that are capable of generating photographs and films for display on computer, television, cinema screens, and other means. Not to mention that a great majority of video games reside under this category. It is now viable to exploit computer programs for producing parts or lengthy scenes of movies, as exemplified by the renowned movie *Toy Story 2*,[4] which was produced completely within a computer-dominated environment. In other words, all characters, scenes, and movie events have been produced and created by the computers utilizing specific software. All versions of the film are stored inside the computer's memory and can be directly displayed from it.[5]

---

4 This is a wonderful American film produced in 2009 using 3-D technology that portrays the adventures of a group of toys that turn real when no humans are present. It was produced by Pixar and directed by Jon Lasseter, Lee Unkrich, and Ash Brannon. The first part was produced in 1999.

5 Ibid, page 444.

IT Projects

IT Projects are the technical, commercial, legal, and financial activities that accompany a certain party's desire to design, develop, and implement an integrated information technology system, governed by a specific contract, as portrayed throughout this book. Information system projects lie in the heart of software, while software resides in the heart of the information industry. Therefore, the word *project* (from a legal and contractual perspective) refers to a specific case or a specific application of software and/or information technology, governed by a concrete contract. Each of these cases possesses a distinctive, pertinent, and protective contract (just as each illness has its remedy).[6] Projects are the essence of industry, in addition to being the practical application of industry and technology. From a contractual panorama, we notice that each project commands an idiosyncratic contract, and it is virtually unequivocal that two projects are never identical. This is where knowledge, cognizance, and dexterity all come into play.

For all the aforementioned reasons and others, without delving into excessively technical details to distinguish between the various terms, and for the purpose of discussing the subject of contracts, we shall utilize the term software and IT in unison as tantamount, where it shall be understood that the aforementioned term includes the word *computer* in its annals. It should be understood, as well, the IT projects encompass upgrades and modifications that are done to the existing or new systems, in addition to projects involving purely technical services, such as professional and consultation service projects, maintenance, and support and software development.

The History of the Software Industry

The *software industry* is relatively younger; in fact a very recent one, if compared to other industries, such as building and construction, which

---

6 In fact, a contract is a potent "remedy" for a "chronic illness" in a world witnessing an increasing rate of failure in software and information system projects, as will be portrayed later.

surfaced as far back as the origins of humankind. Inevitably, Adam and Eve would have built themselves a shelter to reside in, and if we delve deep into the annals of history, more than seven thousand years ago, we see that the Ancient Egyptians had built themselves a most formidable construction that perpetuates to amaze us even today, as one of the wonders of the world. More recently, humankind has erected a structure at the cost of $1.5 billion, which required a period of four years to complete and is considered as the world's tallest building (the Burj Khalifa in Dubai, the United Arab Emirates), as of the time of this printing.

The word *software* first emerged in the United States of America in 1953 but was first utilized during the 1960s.[7] Before that time, software development took place either by the users (customers) themselves or only by selecting a few software companies, such as UNIVAC or renowned IBM. The first company that was purposely established for this end was Computer Usage Company in 1955. Starting from the 1960s, the software industry began to flourish, with the greater promulgation of computers, whether on the production or usage levels and as computers were being mass produced. This expeditious mass production took place in order to gratify the increasing demands by universities, governments, banks, corporations, and entrepreneurs, which created a momentous need for the application software. At that time, the software development and productions used to be done by users themselves, at the hands of programming teams that were designated for that task on a full-time basis. Thereafter, some companies started to embark on selling and marketing both computers and software bundled together (computer plus operating systems plus programming environment).

Thus far, the great leap for the software industry came with the emergence of the personal computer during the seventies, which enabled the world to utilize computers on a large scale. Over subsequent years, software operations flourished notably, and numerous applications and software were produced to cater to an array of sectors and businesses. Computer games were also launched, in addition to service programs

---

[7] It is claimed that Jon W. Turkey was the first to use the term software in 1953. (Source: Wikipedia.)

called utilities, which are general programs that perform diagnoses, maintenance, and rectification services.

At the turn of the current century, a new form of software utilization emerged, that being software as a service (SaaS), whereby software can be accessed through the Internet so the user would not be forced to install the same on his personal computer. This facilitated the use of software at a lower cost and minimized piracy operations as well, to which the software was subjected.[8]

It is greatly acclaimed that the United States is the birthplace of the global software industry. The industry thrived in all its glory through a series of sizeable projects implemented by the US government, the first of which was the SAGE project in 1949. The SAGE project had witnessed a contractual agreement signed by and between the American government and a company vested with the task of developing the information system of the US Air Force. The total contract value amounted to eight million US dollars and was considered by some to be an epic of the software industry,[9] engaging some seven hundred developers from twelve hundred in the entire United States at that time. The project required programming around one million lines of source code and was prolonged from 1949 to 1962.

The second-largest software project in the world was called SABRE and launched in 1954, when American Airlines commissioned IBM to develop its reservations system. With a total cost of $30 million, the project was completed in 1964 and thereafter evolved to embrace a network of travel agencies, whose members totalled thirty thousand, serving some three million travellers. It is said that these two projects resembled the university from which thousands of programmers graduated and embarked on establishing their own corporations, some of which still stand today.

---

8 Robert Bond, Software Contracts: Law, Practice and Precedents (fourth edition), Special Report, Tottel, 2010, page 31.

9 Deltev J. Hoch, Cyriac R. Roeding, Gert purkert and Sandro K. Lindner., "Secrets of Software Success: Management Insights from 100 Software Firms around the World", Harvard Business School Press, 1999.

In 1955, the first company which specialized in developing and producing software worldwide was established by two ex-IBM programmers, Elmer Kubie and John Sheldon, with a capital amount of $40,000. They named their new corporation Computer Usage Company (CUC), which soon expanded to boast some seven hundred programmers by 1967, in addition to possessing twelve offices across the United States. Numerous companies followed suit, and their number skyrocketed to twenty-eight hundred in just twelve years. The scope of work included software development in addition to other related services.

In Europe, the rise of this industry began later than in the United States, when the first such company was established in France in 1958 under the name SEMA, followed by the first company in Britain in 1960, named CAP. Both companies were later then merged in 1988.

Software Categories

The term software incorporates a number of computer programming products that can be grouped together, with respect to the date of emergence, as follows[10]:

- custom-tailored software
- independent software products
- enterprise solutions
- Packaged, mass-marketed software
- Internet and value-added services

In general, the software is an entity that can be contemplated from several angles. One, for instance, software constitutes the fundamental infrastructure for computer operation, called infrastructure software, such as operating systems, middleware, and databases produced by corporations like IBM, Sybase, EMC, Oracle, and VMware. There are other specialized software technologies catering to banking corporations, the manufacturing sector, educational institutions, communication businesses, and others, which are produced by corporations such as Oracle and SAP SE. Perhaps the categories of software are infinite.

10 Ibid. 25.

The grouping of software will definitely be reflected in many ways in the discipline of software and IT contracts, as highlighted in different sections of this book. The key industry frontrunners in the software market include Symantec, Apple, Adobe, IBM, Oracle, and Microsoft, whereas the leading industry associations include:

- Software and Information Industry Association (www.slia.net)
- Software Industry Professionals (www.siprofessionals.org)
- Business Software Alliance. (www.bsa.org)
- Entertainment Software Association (www.theesa.com)
- IAENG Society of Software Engineering (www.iaeng.org//sse.html)

Global Software Market

According to a report compiled through the joint efforts of several researchers (in which some two hundred entrepreneurs and analysts participated worldwide), via the Gartner Project,[11] the performance of the software industry during the second quarter of 2012 far exceeded forecasts. This was at a time when other industries – and the global economy in general – strived to experience numerous challenges and hassles. The industry had reported a business volume valued at approximately $3.6 trillion (globally), at an increase of 3 per cent compared to the previous year, which witnessed a volume amounting to $3.5 trillion, in spite of the economic crisis in Europe and the struggling growth rate in both the United States and China. The report also revealed that expenditure in what is referred to as Public Cloud Services is expected to increase by up to 20 per cent – to around $109 billion – compared to the $91 billion recorded in 2011, and that by 2016, expenditure is set to double, reaching a total of $207 billion. Moreover, the report stipulated that services pertaining to the telecommunications industry will resort to the substantial portion of expenditure in this sector. The report expected expenditures in this domain to hit $1,069 trillion, at an increase of $104

11 Gartner is a renowned international corporation specialized in research and consultation services for the information technology and telecommunications sector. It was founded in 1974, with headquarters in Stanford, Connecticut, and employs some 5500 workers, including 1400 researchers.

billion compared to 2011, with analysts noticing that $864 billion were expended as fees in the domain of technology-related services.

The Importance of the Software Industry

This book is dedicated to scrutinize the difficulties associated with software projects[12] due to the substantial role played by the software in world economies today. Despite this industry being no older than sixty years, it has been developed during this period in such an exceptional and brisk manner that it may be stated that modern civilization cannot be imagined without software. Software is involved in almost every industry and is in control of the vast majority of our lives, from nuclear energy to genetic engineering,[13] through to petroleum, telecommunications, cars, aircraft,[14] banks, shops, and much more. It permeates the economy, commerce, manufacturing, the military, politics, education, entertainment, and many other facets. The world has indeed become addicted to software.[15]

Moreover, software has become a vital element for guiding and amplifying the economic growth worldwide, to an extent that one may claim, "the software industry is the best place to understand the changes that we have to make both, in our business models and in understanding the economy".[16] In addition, a significant portion of global fortunes today revolves around software and its associated

---

12 What is meant here is computer software, or software used on independent computers. This is because software is a product that has been utilized in all industries, even though these are in fact not different from the ones used in other industries. Yet this study focused only on computer-software contracts.

13 It is said that credit for expediting the discovery of the human genetic code should be given to the assistance extended by software experts. Op. cite. *Secrets of Software Success, page 5..*

14 Edward Yourdon, a software expert states, "The huge Boeing 777 that contains four billion highly complex designs could be regarded as a bunch of software with wings" (Op. cite. *Secrets of Software Success*, 5).

15 Op. Cite., 5.

16 Op. cite., 6 (Paul Romanian, an economist at Stanford University, specializes in Growth Theory.)

industries and expertise. Some statistics[17] show, in a survey that included some four hundred millionaires, the software industry in the United States alone produced twenty-two individuals whose fortunes exceeded $300 million. This value exceeds what other numerous paramount industries have produced, such as pharmaceuticals and the food and chemical industries. Another statistics report[18] reveals that the software industry has yielded six out of forty of the world's richest men.

It is claimed that Larry Ellison, the CEO of Oracle who died in 2012, earned around $6.5 million every day (not every year) between April 1997 and April 1998, as an outcome of the increase in the price of corporate share prices. Bill Gates, the founder of Microsoft and the world's wealthiest man from 1995–2009 (excluding 2008), amassed his fortune from the software industry as well. It is asserted moreover that Microsoft Corporation alone created between five thousand and ten thousand millionaires, with this number later increasing to fifty-five. More statistics manifested that whereas the number of millionaires (individuals with fortunes exceeding one million dollars) in the software industry of Silicon Valley in the United States increased by 44 per cent, this rate does not go beyond 7 per cent across the nation.[19]

On the other hand, the software industry during the seventeen years preceding 1997 has achieved top investment opportunities for twelve of the previous seventeen years, vanquishing the PC business, semiconductors, network equipment, and others. Moreover, considering another benchmark and comparing the market value of the company to the market-to-book value, we discover a great irony. This is because software companies recorded the highest market value in comparison to the market-to-book values of all other industries (specifically here we refer to the United States), whereby the ratio was recorded at 1:16 in 1997, which later increased to 1:31. In other industries, such as telecommunications, the ratio was 1:7; in retail commerce, it was recorded as being 1:5; in chemical industries, 1:4; in banks, vehicles, and computer-chip manufacturing, 1:3.

---

17 Op. Cite., 7.

18 Op. Cite., 8.

19 Op. cite., 7

In terms of jobs, the software industry has been and strives to be the largest job creator, for until 1996, more than two million programmers were employed in this industry in the United States alone. Around 95,000 positions become vacant annually and 364 positions remain vacant. A statistical report issued by the Labour Department (USA)[20] asserted that the growth rate in the software industry would remain the highest until 2006. We can here summarize the importance of software in the following:

- The contribution of the software and related services in the overall world economy industry has historically grown faster than the rest of economic sectors.
- The software market is huge and highly globalized. According to some reports (Gartner Project [1]), a solid 6.4 per cent growth in software industry was observed in 2013, with a total industry revenue approaching $300 billion. This brings the overall three-year growth rate for the software industry from 2011 to 2013 to 6.8 per cent. Gartner also envisions the continued future growth in the industry, anticipating software industry revenues will grow to $360 billion by 2016.[21]
- Software and IT industry are leaders in innovation. BSAs[22] publicly traded member companies spent nearly $43 billion on R&D in 2008, equal to their collective revenue.
- Software drives productivity and innovation in almost every economic sector, thus providing an aid to businesses of all sizes to perform better. Some fifteen industry users of IT include manufacturing, telecom, financial services, construction, health care, and utilities.[23]

But that's not all. Software forms the backbone of the most important technological development of the twentieth century, that being the Internet, which is a wonder that could not have been brought about had it not been for software. It is these computer programs that have facilitated the means of communication between millions of people, which takes

---

[20] Op. Cite. 9.

[21] Clay Brown, 2013 Software Industry Trends.

[22] Business Software Allaince.

[23] Information Technology Foundation USA.

credit for devising new social media channels and mechanisms, as exemplified by Facebook, Twitter, Nexopis, and many others.

The Ferocious and Rebellious Nature of Software

In spite of the great significance of this ingenious product, the software industry is often described as being one of the most intricate entities created by man of all time. This is due to the idiosyncratic nature the software industry owns, for it is a surreal world, a utopia that does not yet exist. Meanwhile, software can be described as being rather ferocious and rebellious. Many of the writers in the field have trumpeted this fact that failure has become a trait accompanying software and information system projects, or that software development is, in fact, "mission impossible",[24] or its projects "are subjected to failure",[25] or these projects almost "always have one thing in common: failure".[26]

Phil Simon said, "In more than a decade of working on different IT projects countries and industries, I almost invariably saw the same outcome each time: some type of IT project failure". He added: "Many enterprise system implementations failed despite the presence of many attributes conducive to success: generous IT budget, relatively mature applications, consulting firms with significant expertise, and thousands of previous projects to serve an examples and cautionary tales. Yet most of these projects continued to fail".[27]

Indeed, the flipside of this unique coin could at first be rather astonishing. If we were to examine this scrupulously, we would sniff out diversified reasons (as viewed by some) for this failure: one of such ground reasons is the source code, especially when large and complex, and is composed

---

24 «Software Development: Completing the Mission Impossible" (Op. cite. Secrets of Software Success, 93).

25 «So Prone to Failure" (Ibid. 94).

26 «One Thing in Common: Failure" (Ibid. 94).

27 Phil Simon is an independent technology consultant and the author of Why New Systems Fail, an excellent source used extensively in this book. Phil is also the author of The Next Wave of Technology. The above quotation is from his book "Why New Systems Fail", xxv.

of millions of (programming) lines. A program such as Windows 95, for instance, comprises of some eleven million programming lines, and each of these contains at least one effective command that influences the rest. It therefore must interact with the other lines, meaning that even a single minute error in any one of these lines could result in the failure of the entire program. This is in addition to the extensive interaction between the program's modules, whereby any malfunction in any part of the program will inevitably affect the remaining parts.

Moreover, software – being designed and produced in a virtual world – is shrouded in a great deal of *uncertainty and unpredictability*, compared to other industries. This is due to several reasons, one being the obliviousness of users regarding the definite needs and requirements at the time of signing the contract, leading to a later stage for continuous modification and changes of software. This is considered one of the most acute complications to deal with, in software projects, since it entails the need for more time, resources, and thus additional cost. Also and until recently, there was no way for ensuring the validity or correctness of software design, coupled with the ongoing change in the technology infrastructure in which the program operates, as well as the change in other software owned by various parties. An error in predicting the time required and budget needed for executing the project goes to put the developers and vendors involved under time pressure, making them more prone to committing errors. This may be a terrible recipe resulting in disaster.

Is There Any Perfect Software or IT Systems?

This unique nature of software was the reason for many commentators, writers, and large number of members of the software industry to argue that "eliminating defects effectively from software is impossible for so many reasons"[28], the following reasons are only some:

---

[28] Diane Rowland, Uta Kohl and Andrew Charlesworth, Information Technology Law, Fourtth Eddition, Routledg, tayler & Francis Group, page 436.

- Modern software packages are simply too complex, and have to interact with computer operating systems and many other applications, as well as a range of hardware produced by different manufacturers, and the discrepancies in environment that result from this make it impossible to ensure an accurate performance of software package in all circumstances.
- Simply, it is commercially unrealistic for software vendors to attempt to eliminate all software defects prior to delivery. They would rather prefer to deliver defective software subject beta testing as a more effective way to avoid potential liability, rather than seeking to produce perfect software.[29]
- This is especially the case when these projects entail transforming ideas into deliverables and systems operating in the real world, and they are designed and implemented primarily in an illusionary world.

This fact has been recognized by one of the most famous US legislations known as the "uniform computer information transaction act" (UCITA)[30], which sought to produce such a one-size-fits-all approach for computer software contracting by saying, "Indeed, a perfect program may not be possible at all". According to Phil Simon: "Assuming zero errors and delay-free projects is downright foolish".[31]

Management of Software Projects

Before delving deeper, let us have a brisk overview of an important topic that diligently relates to the subject matter of this book; that is, *software project management*, which might be one of the culprits of persistently low success rates on these projects. Being one of the branches of the science of project management, IT project management combines management and engineering. It involves developing the means and methods of project management, insofar as accurate planning and

29 Ibid, 437.

30 Available at www.law.upnn.edu/bll/archives/ulc/ucita/ucita200/pdf

31 Phil Smith, Ibid, 317.

execution monitoring conforms to the estimated budget, the designated time, and the required quality.

The rebellious nature of software, which deems it difficult to control or direct and as outlined in the previous paragraph, must inevitably reflect on the management of IT and software projects, making these too a challenge to contend with.

Failure of Software and IT Projects

In spite of the great importance commanded by the software industry today, there exists a curious phenomenon accompanying this significance, which is then exemplified by an increase in failure rates in implementing software and IT projects. This has become apparent through numerous studies conducted in the United States and other countries. What is truly remarkable is that pondering over the importance of software and information technology in this age, and their pivotal role in increasing productivity; business development; industrial and human advancement; their apparent manifestation of scientific and technological progress; and their culmination of human intellect and creativity, the undeniable fact is; failure rate of these projects yet remains considerably high.

Although the subject of IT projects faileur is too larg and and propbly exceeds the purview of this book, however following are some authenticated and documented statics prving the above fact:

Chaos Report (1995)

One of the most prominent researches examining the success rate of software and IT projects, was conducted by the firm Standish Group, which is a designated American research company specializing in the studies and research pertaining to software and information technology. The firm issues annual reports outlining the success and failure rates of software projects in the United States, under **"The Chaos Report".** The first report was published in 1995 and is considered a prominent indicator in the failure of software and IT projects. This report was an outcome of a survey conducted on a number of executive IT managers working in companies of all sizes (large, medium and small) across various sectors and industries (banks, securities, retail and wholesale, insurance, services, local and federal). 365 executive managers were surveyed and they spoke about 8,380 software applications; in addition to the one-to-one interviews conducted. The results of the survey came as an outright shock, since the number of projects said to have been cancelled prior to completion constituted 31.1% and 52.7% of projects cost 189% of their original estimated budget. The report mentioned that this sizeable cost constituted only "the tip of the proverbial iceberg" as the saying goes, *since the cost of missed opportunities is immeasurable and could reach trillions of Dollars in the United States alone.* The firm estimated that companies and government agencies in the United States in the year 1995 had spent a total of *81 billion dollars* on software and IT projects that were cancelled prior to completion.

It also stated that these companies and agencies were compelled to spend a further $59 billion to get their projects completed, at both a higher cost and a longer duration. The report put the number of cancelled projects in 1995 at approximately eighty thousand.

As for the success stories, the report indicated that only *16.2 per cent* of projects were successfully accomplished within budget and time limits, while the success rates of large projects were much worse, accounting for only *9 per cent.* Even with those projects completed successfully (within time and budget), many failed to accomplish their proposed functions and specifications, as originally agreed. According to the report, large companies achieved only 42 per cent of these functions and specifications, whereas in small companies this amounted to 78.4 per cent of projects.

In another study, the results of which were startling at the time, was conducted in the same year (1995) on some eight thousand software projects in the United States, publicized this fact that *84 per cent* of these projects do not finish on time, within budget and have only some features installed. In 30 per cent of all projects, the contract was terminated and the project was cancelled prior to completion. Another study found that more than 50 per cent of the large and complex projects were cancelled prematurely, and the losses resulting from the failure of these software projects in 1995 were amounted to *1 billion dollars.*[32]

Yet another study also conducted in the United States figured out that 75 per cent of the large-scale computer projects (where source program lines exceeded sixty-four thousand) encountered considerable difficulties and risks during implementation, where three hundred errors emerged for every one thousand original program lines. Two per cent of these projects were utterly collapsed and were terminated, whereas 60 per cent of the projects overshot allotted budgets and timeframes, with the average delay experienced exceeded one year at approximately double the cost, at times.[33]

2001

In 2001, The Standish Group published the report of a study conducted on thirty thousand projects during a period spanning six years (1994 to 2000), whose results were as follows:

- In 1994, the project success rates did not exceed 18 per cent, with the remainder distributed between complete failure (24 per cent) and partial failure (58 per cent).
- In 1996, the success rate was recorded to be 22 per cent, with the remainder distributed between complete failure (40 per cent) and partial failure (38 per cent).
- In 1998, the project success rates did not exceed 22 per cent, with the remainder distributed between complete failure (24 per cent) and partial failure (54 per cent).
- In 2000, things were still not looking up, since project success rates did not exceed 23 per cent, with the remainder distributed between complete failure (20 per cent) and partial failure (57 per cent). The study categorized "successful projects" as those completed successfully within designated budget and expected

[32] Richard Raysman and Peter Brown, *Computer Law: Drafting and Negotiating Forms and Agreements*, 2004, Law Journal seminars-press. Page 2.07.

[33] Ibid, 2.07.

period, while achieving the required functions and specifications. "Failed projects" were specified as the ones that were cancelled or not implemented, whereas "challenged projects" were implemented, albeit exceeding time and budget constraints and achieving only a part of their intended functions.

The study attributed failure to a number of reasons, including poor project planning, ambiguity of objectives, persistent alterations in project goals, unrealistic estimation of time, and other required resources lack of support by those responsible coupled with absence of user participation, lost team spirit, and skill deficiencies. The study also asserted that large projects were more prone to failure than the smaller ones, due to the complex technical nature of the former.[34]

According to the report, in 1994, a total investment of $250 billion was made on IT projects, in the United States, from which $140 billion were lost, $80 billion of which in completely failed projects.

Robbins–Gioia

In a study survey conducted by Robbins-Gioia (an American institution specializing in rendering management consultation services, based in the state of Virginia in 2001, it was revealed that 36 per cent of 232 companies representing numerous sectors were in the process of executing enterprise resource planning (ERP) projects. Following enlisted results were unearthed in this study:

- 51 per cent of the participants put forward the notion that the ERP implementation was a failure.
- 46 per cent of participants noted that despite the system being implemented, they were not convinced that it would improve the business at their corporation.

[34] The Robbins–Gioia Survey (2001).

2004

Standish Group issued a report revealing a remarkable improvement of success rates, reached by software and IT projects (still concerning the United States), compared to the first report that was released in 1994. Specifically, the success rate after ten years (and based on a study that was conducted on forty thousand projects) reached up to 34 per cent, which is almost double the percentage mentioned in the first report. Jim Johnson, the Standish Group CEO, stated that the reason for this improvement was the trend towards reducing project size, adopting new alternative process management techniques (different from the conventional "waterfall method"), and increase in the awareness of users and project managers.

2008

In 2008, based on the USA prominent study which was conducted by the US government for the purpose of improving "the management of information technology (IT) investments": planning, management and oversight of the IT projects amounting to billions of dollars". The study was supervised by two governmental agencies. First was the US Government Accountability Office (GAO), a state agency operating as the arm of the US Congress in the field of surveys and studies; and the second was the office of management and budget (OMB), a federal agency playing a pivotal role in the field of monitoring and supervising the Federal government's investments. The study focused on two types of projects: the ones under the management watch list, and the ones that were categorized as high-risk projects. The study came up with the following results:

- It was revealed that around 413 IT projects existed, with a sum of at least $25.2 billion in expenditures of fiscal year 2008. These were either poorly planned or poorly performed, or both. OBM determined that 352 projects (at a total cost of about $23.4 billion) were poorly planned. However, 78 poorly performed projects (with a total $4.8 billion) existed, which pertained to the second type (i.e. high-risk projects), while 26 projects at a total value of $3 billion were categorized as both *poorly planned* and *poorly performed.*

- The study uncovered as well, that 48 per cent of federal government projects in the IT field "have been "rebase lined'[35] for several reasons, incorporating alterations in project goals and funding. Fifty-one per cent of those projects were rebase lined at least twice, and about 11 per cent were rebase lined four times or more"[36].

2011

A recent survey that was conducted in 2011 by software company Geneca was titled "Doomed from the Start". The survey consisted of twenty-five closed-ended questions and was brought to a conclusion by 596 individuals meticulously involved in the software development process. The survey revealed the following key findings:

- Lack of confidence in project success: 75 per cent of the respondents admitted their projects were either always or usually "doomed right from the start".
- Rework wariness: 85 per cent admitted they spent at least half their time on rework.
- Inconsistent business involvement resulted in confusion: 78 per cent felt the business was usually or always out of sync with project requirements, and business stakeholders needed to be more involved and engaged in the requirement process.

Recent Examples

Examples portraying the failure of IT projects are abundant, whether worldwide or within the Middle East (ME) region. Among the most prominent of these examples, which has been meticulously documented

---

35 This expression means that the basics and main elements of the project has been redesigned or redrafted.

36 See the full report and contents of the study online (GAO-08-1051T).

on a global level,[37] is the virtual case file project. This was a project being executed for the FBI,[38] whose failure leads to the loss of $170 million, and to the squandering of five full years. The fire control project (2007) is another example from the United Kingdom, the project targeting the UK Fire and Rescue System by replacing forty-six local control rooms with a network of nine purpose-built regional control centres. The project was expected to be accomplished in October 2009, the original estimated cost £120 million. By 2009, two years into the project, the expected duration of the project had doubled and the anticipated total project cost had increased by 500 per cent to £635 million. In 2010, the contract was terminated, after a sum of £469 million had been wasted.

Conclusion

The great eminence of the software industry in every aspect of our life has been tempered with the fact that there is no software free of error. These types of amazing paradoxes and other factors truly make the world of software a unique, ferocious, and rebellious one. No wonder then the software and IT projects are significantly surrounded by unpredictability and exposure. According to John F. Keane, the founder of a billion-dollar professional software services firm who has spent thirty years in the industry: "It's also like riding a bull. You really have to be aware of the bull's movements, because every time you think you succeed, you are thrown off the bull".[39]

====================

[37] In this regard, we refer to a new realm of law titled "Preventive Law", which is a unique branch seeking to prevent the occurrence of disputes at the outset using preventive steps and measures. It is founded on a grand idea, which preaches that the best usage of legal knowledge is before problems unfold (i.e. to prevent their occurrence or mitigate them). Credit should be given to Louis Brown, the father of this new branch of law, for laying the groundwork.

[38] Federal Bureau of Investigation

[39] Op. Cite., 317.

Chapter 2
WHY IT PROJECTS FAIL?

Aim of the Chapter

As depicted in the previous chapter, the risk and exposure in IT projects is extremely high, as proved by statistics and reports presented. This chapter moves further to answer an easy but abstract question: why IT projects fail. The answer may flow easily when we analyse the types of risks involved and associated with such projects, and then how to use such analysis to propose a new approach that may help to control such risks.

Background

Prior to inspecting the reasons and causes for failure, we should first familiarize ourselves with IT projects failure definition. It is to be noted also that failure is not based on one degree but several. In general, the project will be stigmatized as "failed" when overrunning the budget and/or the schedule by certain degrees (usually 15–30 per cent) and/or failing to demonstrate the same percentage of the planned and intended benefits. In particular, the status of a project can be classified into three categories:

a. Successful: The projects that were completed on time and on budget, with all features and functions that were initially specified.
b. Failed: The ones that were cancelled before completion or never implemented.
c. Challenged: Incorporates the projects that were completed and operational, but over budget, over time, and comprise a few of the features initially specified.

One well known writer in this field, Phil Simon, groups the failure of software and IT projects into four categories[40] as follows:

- "The Unmitigated Disaster" are projects that have met with complete and utter failure. These are projects that exhausted budgets without receiving any IT system in return, with the possibility of being disputed in a court of law.
- "Big Failure" projects have exceeded in cost at least double what was planned and an implementation time exceeding double the agreed-upon timeframe. These projects belong to the systems that completely fail to perform the required functions.
- "Mild Failure" projects are those feebly exceeding the time and budget limits, but not extensively, while not achieving all intended purposes.
- "Forthcoming Failure" projects are doomed to fail, owing to their erroneous assumptions, incorrect data/information,

[40] Phil Simon, Op.Cite, page 8.

inadequate documentation, or on which users have not been sufficiently trained.

Therefore, it becomes apparent that simple and primary failure criteria involve the *project exceeding its estimated time and budget limits, or that the project falls short of performing its functions.* The degree of failure will be varied based on the extension of deviation from the original estimated time, cost, and agreed-upon functions.

Why IT Projects Fail

This phenomenon has caught the attention of many researchers. They have perceived that the reasons underlying the high rate of failure, as indicated by the aforementioned studies and numerous others, is due to various reasons. Some are related to the provider or developer and others belong to the client, while still others pertain to the nature of software industry itself, as it revolves around a number of factors that are difficult to control and predict.

One of the reasons is associated with human resources specifically, because the staff turnover in the IT industry is extensive. Some trained developers depart during the implementation of any given phase of a project without a back-up plan in place, which results in relinquishing the skilled professionals or replacing him or her with less experienced ones. This occurs on both sides, the provider as well as the client. Thus, it negatively influences the progress of the project.

Another reason for failure is the constant requests for modification by customers during the project and lack of their cooperation, insofar as providing the needed information and clearances at the right time. Moreover, the provider might contribute to the failure by inaccurate estimation of his technical capabilities, resources, or time required to complete the job.

Here I would like to refer to some related insights:

- The causes for failure can be anticipated and predicted at any stage of the project, but unfortunately, many can happen without any notice. An example of this is the problem discovered during the data migration, or during system testing or system integration and many other such as the change in the political environment or vendor economic collapse.
- The seed of failure can be found in any stage of the project cycle, pre-implementation, during the implementation, or even after the system activation.
- In the view of some writers, the picture can be much gloomier where the budget and deadline are not only the two criteria for IT project failure. There is what is called "latent failure": the project has met its objectives in terms of budget and time but still suffers from problems that appear only after activation in the area of documentation, data, and processing.
- On the other hand, all IT projects are unique, no two face identical challenges, and many factors make each implementation standalone cases.
- Organizations usually try to hide the failures of a system's implantation.

Reasons for failure or success may be summarized by the results revealed by a study, conducted on a number of large- and medium-sized projects in Kuwait[41] [42] and some other countries in the Middle East as follows:

Failure Factors

- ☒ Absence of a party assuming responsibility on the project
- ☒ Absence of sufficient human resources for executing the project
- ☒ Client has no or little conviction regarding the project's significance
- ☒ Lack of accurate planning and analysis

41

42 [41] Saad Al-Barrak, "Success and Failure of Information Systems: A Supplier's Perspective", The London School of Management (Royal Holloway), January 2001, 384..

- ☒ Upper management not providing the necessary support and backing
- ☒ Users not participating in the project
- ☒ Absence of adequate assistance by the main providers
- ☒ Failure attributes within the project itself: extremely complex, difficult to use, absence of specific monitoring procedures, high cost, numerous technical difficulties, intangible benefits, ambiguous outputs, inappropriate or outdated devices
- ☒ End users' dissatisfaction with the project
- ☒ No cooperation between provider and the IT department
- ☒ Improper project management
- ☒ Internal administrative problems affecting the customer

Success Factors

- ☑ Strong support provided by management
- ☑ Sound support and assistance from providers
- ☑ Efficient project management
- ☑ The existence of a real need for the project
- ☑ Presence of a responsible party for the project
- ☑ Accurate project planning as exemplified by the existence of a preliminary feasibility study, accurate requirements, accurate preparation of RFP document, meticulous selection of providers, high-quality project, competent project manager
- ☑ Users trained in utilizing the system
- ☑ Enabling the users to take an active part in the project
- ☑ Complete satisfaction of all users
- ☑ System meets expectations
- ☑ Existence of an interest in the project on a national level
- ☑ Strong support and assistance from the IT department
- ☑ Competent project management team
- ☑ Commitment to project success:
- ☑ The capability of resolving problems confronting the project
- ☑ Collaboration and mutual understanding with providers
- ☑ Availing the human resources required by the project and wisely handling any dispute or disagreement with vendors, partners and resources

Risk Definition

A risk in general is defined as the potential that a chosen action or activity (including the choice of inaction) will lead to a loss (an undesirable outcome). The potential losses themselves may also be called risks and thus warrant specific procedures to avoid, mitigate, or divert it altogether.

My own definition of the risks in software and IT projects is any factor that may:

a. directly or indirectly disturb or cause disturbance in any way to the normal process of the project towards its completion, and will adversely affect the time, cost, and quality of the project, as originally agreed between the parties;
b. also lead to or cause dispute escalation between parties. Here we note that this study focuses on the contracting phase where we believe that many of the seeds of failure and success are thrown into the soil of the project at this stage.

Risk Management

Risk management is an important discipline of business administration and involves examining the potential risks that may confront a business activity in any given country at any time instant. Risk management can be defined as a set of organized and meticulous operations that are designed to assist companies and organizations in *identifying* risk positions, *analysing* these risks, *evaluating* their extent, and thus *treating* them appropriately, either by accepting them, taking certain measures to prevent or avoid them, if possible, or mitigating and diverting them. This topic has become one of the most discussed and researched subjects in the field of IT, owing to the following reasons:

1. The most important and detrimental of those reasons is what we mentioned previously, namely the incredible high rate of failure afflicting these types of projects. It is as if the seeds of failure are

sown into the soil of these projects, which warrants everyone involved to work towards improving project success.

2. The increased dependence on software, IT, and relevant services in various industries, coupled with the permeation of software and IT into all fields and facets of life.
3. Perpetually increasing expansion of this industry. We know, for instance, that software and information systems were not considered independent of computer equipment until 1960, when IBM started charging separate fees for software consultation, maintenance, and training. Accordingly, software and computer equipment were looked upon separately, in addition to being considered components of an "information system". Today, services pertaining to the software are not solely confined to maintenance, technical support, and training but extend to incorporate new forms of services such as outsourcing, disaster recovery, escrow, OSS, SoS, Cloud Computing and others.
4. Of course with this expansion and emergence of new forms of service, the rise of intellectual property rights of software and information systems, being knowledge assets of great economic value, was observed. However, this was accompanied by increasing risks and dangers as well.
5. The intensified risks as the software and IT industry becomes increasingly intricate, particularly for systems that run sizeable airports, control complicated air traffic, manage hospitals, and maintain medical records, defence systems, and software that manages warfare and weapons. This is not to mention the world of finance, business, the stock market, commercial transactions, international and local telecommunication networks, and more. Hence, the risks increase for both the provider and the user.
6. The global nature of this field and the fiercely competitive environment dominating the information systems market today. This is in addition to the interrelated commercial ties linking providers to users across the globe.
7. Upon embarking on any IT project, it is necessary to consider various potential risks involved, while accurately balancing the cost of managing these risks or mitigating their impact. It is better yet to avoid them altogether and eradicate the possible

damage that could occur from ignoring them. This may require opting to accept some of these risks, but with full knowledge.

8. In the realm of commerce – indeed, business in general – there exists an acceptable degree of risk, since any human endeavour carries some risk and likewise no business activity is without risks. No business environment exists without risk. On this premise, when we discuss risk management we mean attempting to avoid these risks or mitigating the damage that could be caused in this regard.
9. What is curious (and somewhat perplexing) is that the majority of risks and their reasons are almost known beforehand by the many who are involved, so there are no clear causes for ignoring them. What is even more amazing is that many of these risks are clear and simple and can be detected early enough and to be remedied before any damage is done. As an example, the recent global financial crisis that emanated from the United States in 2009, later spreading to all parts of the world, was clear and obvious for many of the specialists and analysers beforehand.

Types of Risk

In general terms, types of risks can be seen from different perspectives. However, we can classify them at least from three different perspectives:

1. Technical, commercial, and legal
2. Software nature, software contracts, sales cycle
3. Project phases

A. Technical, Commercial, and Legal

A. **Technical** – the aspects of technology related to and associated with IT projects, such as issues pertaining to software and system design and development, implementation and testing, and the customization required to accommodate the needs of clients. Includes issues related to data cleansing and security, data integrity and migration, and source code issues. Includes those related to the integration of the new technology with the existing ones, chosen methodologies of managing the project, products and services' maturity and quality, technical capability of the vendor in project planning and implementation, and many others.

B. Commercial – the business and financial aspects of the project, such as the commercial and overall project evaluation and visibility, arranging the relations with third parties, solvency of either party, cost control, taxation issues, commercial issues involving means of utilizing and marketing the software commercially, qualifying and training software developers on sales and marketing skills, managing human resources, etc.

C. Legal – such as selecting the appropriate legal document to carry out the work, choosing the contract binding both parties and setting contractual conditions and responsibilities, intellectual property rights, liability and limitation of liability, responsibilities, indemnity, warranties and representations, applicable law and dispute resolution, and many others.

Table 1: Areas of Risk from Conventional Respects (Legal, Technical, and Commercial)

Legal (Legal Consultants)	Technical (Technicians and Specialists)	Commercial (Executives, Financiers, and Salesmen)
- Contract parties	- Technical proposal	- Project planning
- Contract form	- Scope of work	- Terms of tender
- Contract drafting - Version control - Documents priority	- Deliverables - Customer Requirements	- Importance and need for the project
- Schedules - Documentation	- Contract Duration - Time extension and renewal	- Risk identification, and overall risk management

- Warranties and representations - Penalties for late delivery - Parties' responsibilities - Parties' liabilities	- Technical schedules - Product maturity - Quality assurance - Data issues - Technology Used - Project management methodology	- Setting project objectives - Resources availability - Cost control - Communication with other party
- Due Diligence	- Criteria for project completion	- Financial proposal
		- Management's conviction of the project
	- System design	- Parties solvency and financial credibility
- IPRs (patent)	- Technical specification - Software customization	- Project financing - Supply, procumbent
- Ownership of software (customized and interfaces)	- Source code - Acceptance tests	- Currency fluctuations - Performance securities
- Software users	- Integration with existing systems	- Relationship with 3rd parties
- Licensing	- Change requests	- Political and economic conditions
	- Additional services	- Required governmental clearances
- Additional agreements and contracts	- Maintenance and managed services - Others	- Logistics - Parties overall reputation - penalties

- Confidentiality		- HR management
- Termination		- Contract value
- Suspension of contract		- Payments terms
- Exit strategies		- Expenses/Fees
- Force majeure		- Taxation - Compliance Others
- Limitation of liability		- Parties awareness of cyber security, export control, anti-corruption and bribery regulations
- Source code escrow		- others
- Legal conditions		
- Applicable laws		
- Dispute resolution - Others		

This is only a preliminary list, which may of course be modified and amended according to the circumstances, the size of the project, the nature of the deliverables and products of each separate project, and the overall environment where the project will be executed. Each of the contracting parties may review the above checklist, analyse it and determine the degree of risk for each point (very high, high, moderate, low, very low, acceptable), its probability and thus decide whether it would be feasible to move forward with the project, and under what type of precaution measurements.

Key Point: As mentioned before, the successful project is a result and the product of cooperation and collaboration of business, legal and technical individuals of both parties who sincerely enjoy the teamwork spirit. A comprehensive analysis of the risk involved cannot be reached without such cooperation.

B. Nature of Software, Software Contracts, and Sales Cycle

After dividing the risks into legal, technical, and financial categories, we can then consider them from another perspective and distinguish between the two risky areas present in various software and IT projects. In spite of the correlation and overlap between these areas, we can still differentiate between them. In this context, we may also distinguish between two tools that could be utilized effectively to keep those risks at bay or to mitigate their impact. What is important is that each phase or area mentioned above possesses a unique nature, condition, and guarantee that must be meticulously scrutinized and taken into consideration by those involved.

Software Nature

This emanates from the rebellious and ferocious nature of software, indeed the nature of their projects, since – as previously outlined – they involve a great degree of uncertainty, whether during the design or in the implementation phase. This area is characterized by its dominantly technical nature, and usually encompasses the risks pertaining to software and IT project management, which is often the culprit for the failure of many projects.

To be fair, two cases can be made in defence of the high degree of risk in this area: the first is the novelty of the industry and its projects in comparison to other industries – such as construction – and second, the invisible and intangible nature of software and, accordingly, its related projects. Often the two parties will enter into an agreement over intangible products or systems that neither has previously seen.[43] The statistics mentioned throughout this book highlight that the failure rate afflicting conventional projects is high, albeit with a slight recent improvement.

The root cause of this specific area is comprised of the following:

- Inaccurate scope or system description

---

43 Harry Beckwith (1997), *Selling the Invisible,* New York: Warner Books.

- Scope creep (expanding and adding to the project scope)
- Dysfunction or inaccuracy of system design
- Unrealistic implementation plan
- Inadequate integration with other systems
- Lack of a sound plan for testing and accepting the system
- Lack of a sound plan for data migrating from the old system to the newer one
- Unqualified and insufficient human resources
- Incompetent project manager
- Lack of control due to project size

Key Point: The risk-breaking tool for this phase would be the full awareness of both parties to the nature of the software and industry, most important, the same to be reflected in the contract governing the project.

Contract

What is meant by the contract is not merely the document signed by both parties at the conclusion of negotiations but the overall theoretical legal principles under which that contract is built. Moreover, a complete contractual process that commences with announcing the project, bidding, receiving proposals, evaluating, and finalizing all related technical and financial documentation, including the related legal documents (such as correspondences, letters of intent, confidentiality agreements and subcontracting contracts).

The risks in this area include, among other things:

The contract (the legal document itself). This risk is brought about by two factors:

1. The absence of an actual contract document. Some projects have begun without the presence of a signed contract, a document that outlines the rights, obligations and responsibilities of the parties. In fact, I have seen projects that have commenced and terminated (in failure) without the parties signing any form of formal legal document.

2. Even with the existence of a contract, it is not adequately "fair, tight, coherent, and robust", as depicted through the following:
   - The contract (or the document) signed by both parties is non-binding, such as a non-binding letter of intent, or both parties signed an incorrect form of the contract, just as if the parties had merely signed a "licensing contract" for a turnkey system.
   - The contract does not include a detailed description of the relevant scope of the project, or it may contain a description that is ambiguous and difficult to interpret. Conversely, the description may lack detail, or be inaccurate or inapplicable.
   - The contract does not contain a detailed description of the deliverables.
   - The contract does not clearly state the responsibilities and obligations of each party.
   - Project management approach or methodology has not been outlined.
   - The clauses emphasizing the significance of cooperation between the parties are lacking.
   - The ownership of intellectual property rights is not specified.
   - One of the parties to the contract is excessively burdened by commitments and obligations (penalties, liability) the financial burden placed on the provider, which may cause the whole project to collapse.
   - Contracting with a client marred by clear financial problems, administrative issues or partner disputes.
   - Absence of a definite mechanism for applying changes to the scope of work during project progress.
   - Absence of a clear mechanism for resolving any disputes that may arise during the contract duration or upon its termination for any reason.
   - Absence of an accurate mechanism for exit strategies during contract duration, expiration or termination.
   - The guarantees and warranties provided by either party are unclear.

Key Point: The risk-breaking tool for this phase would be the construction of a proper, fair, tight, coherent, and robust contract, as we shall outline later.

Taking this point further: I personally believe the risk resides in many people not being aware of the existence of this specific area of law (software and IT contracts), and how to properly utilize them in this context, whereas the contract is in fact a significant tool of success, if utilized correctly in IT projects. As far as the general theory of "law of contract", the contract is the most important source of obligation within the realm of commercial activity, in addition to being a viable tool for guaranteeing success in business, commercial relation, and protecting one's interests.

This is because the contract may be used as a means for outlining and clarifying all issues and details pertaining to the project, and for preventing problems from occurring at the outset. A contract, for instance, may be utilized for accurately describing the "system" or the complete and accurate scope of the project, and thus avoiding problems and disputes that could arise in this regard.

A contract is also a potent mean for distributing risks among all parties fairly. It meticulously outlines the rights and obligations of each, it is important for protecting intellectual property rights of parties, as well as being a protective tool in case any of the parties fails to fulfil its agreed obligations. In my opinion, there is nothing to prevent employing the contract in this capacity, save perhaps the lack of appreciation for legal counsels by entrepreneurs, or the lack of expertise by legal consultants when it comes to the milieu or nature of IT projects, or both. Needless to say, it is precisely the unique nature of software and IT projects that has necessitated the presence of tailored contracts, and the availability of specialized and designated individuals to deal with them.

Sales Cycle

Among the risky domains found in software and IT projects, as I see it, are the sales cycle and the expertise of salesmen, technicians and project managers in this industry. The sales cycle typically passes through four distinct phases, whereby a defect, occurring in any one of these phases, sows the seeds for failure and could derail the entire project.

Key point: An important tool for circumventing the risks in this area lies in the company possessing a robust *internal policy* that clearly outlines the sales cycle, together with a sales team commitment for every phase. A clear, understandable procedure and regulation for *contract administration* must be carefully chosen as well, to deal with agreements, purchase orders, and authorized signatories. We should also refer here to the significance of arranging a proper *educational program* for business and technical staff. Building the basic *legal knowledge of the sales team* in the field of IT (and others) is a focal point overlooked by many. These individuals must be made familiar with the principles of contracting for software and IT projects, risks and exposure associated with IT projects, basic principles of contracts, their components and legal weight, in addition to programs' pertinent intellectual property rights, the limits of liability, sales cycles, their phases, importance, impact, and legal bearing.

Table 2: Risks from Different Perspectives

Risk Area	Remedy	Tool
Nature of Software and IT Projects	- Accurate system description - Accurate description of scope of work - Realistic time schedule - Competent human resources - Customer cooperation - Project management approach - Wise scientific management - Project governance and control - Not to start the project early	IT Contract
Software and IT Contracts	- Choosing correct contract form - Formulating a robust contract - Using the contract as a means to "codify" project elements - Complete conviction and belief in the project - Examining and specifying risks - Clearly outlining the rights and responsibilities and liabilities of each party - Outlining the penalties of violation by either party - Sound project planning - Change control mechanism	IT Contract

Sales Cycle	- Sales team familiar with the contract's basic legal aspects - Importance of maintaining the contract administration policy for sales and contracts - Sales team firm understands dealings and legal relations between the parties (subcontractors, third parties) - Understanding the different types of legal components (letter of intent, confidentiality agreement, subcontracts, etc.) - Adhere to the contract administration policy	Company Policies

C. Projects Phases

The risks in software and IT projects can also be perceived from the process of contracting for IT projects and project phase, as follows:

Pre-Contractual Phase

In this phase, the client announces the desire for new system, and issues its vision of the system desired and the terms and condition that has to be considered by the bidders. In response to this desire, the providers submit their proposals. Once received by the client, the same will be subjected to examination and evaluation. This phase ends by awarding the project to the winner among the competing providers. The significance of this phase relies gathering the business requirements in this stage are one of the most important activity.

The risk here lies in not meticulously or correctly reading the tender document; misinterpretation by technicians and sales team of project technicalities, scope, inputs and outputs, technologies and applicability; incorrect elucidation of the client needs and requirements; misunderstanding the client business requirements; erroneous estimation of project cost, resources and time required for implementation; inadequate regulation of the third party relations by not signing the necessary agreements and establishing appropriate legal relationships; or the two parties not becoming sufficiently familiar with one another; or that the parties were not introduced to the technical capabilities and financial aptitude of one another. The situation will apparently be more worth if the tender is for projects outside the local boarder. The lack of information about doing business cross the boarders represents a high degree of risk and simply can lead to a disaster.

Contracting Phase

I believe this is the paramount phase, where the approach adopted by this book is focused. It is core to the project's success. In this phase, the parties go to the insights of the project and try to reach an accurate and common understanding for the scope of the project: who will do what, when, and how. They will also try to predict every future possibility, and devise a solution to difficulties they may encounter during the project. After they make sure they are insync and understand each other perfectly, they write what they have agreed to on paper. Upon signing, it is often considered the only reference. There exists abundant risks in this phase, which are usually overlooked by both parties. The legal document (i.e. the project contract) is the best remedy to overcoming those risks, provided the contract is a coherent, robust, and balanced one, as suggested by the new approach.

Project Implementation Phase

The risks here involve the absence of a designated department for managing software and IT projects; the lack of adequate human and financial resources for implementation; the absence of a professional and accurate mechanism for documenting project execution; the continuous changes to project scope and specifications; the nonexistence of a sound mechanism dealing with changes occurring during implementation; lack of a dispute-resolution mechanism; no appropriate procedures for exit strategies where necessary; the absence of qualified and competent personnel for managing and executing the project; and lack of proper reporting channels to monitor the progress of the project.

Post-Implementation Phase (Warranty, Maintenance, and Technical Support)

The major risk here is the absence of a clear vision of the provider's commitments during the warranty and maintenance phase earlier in advance, or lack of correct anticipation on the part of client for the human and financial needs required for system operation.[44]

The following table outlines the risks that are persistent in software projects from a different perspective – that being the phases through which the project passes.

Table 3: Risks from the Perspective of Project Phases

Phase	Risk	Procedures
Pre—Contract	Inattentive reading or comprehending the tender terms Organization is not ready for the new system (resources and business process) Poor documentation/lack of adequate documentation of what has been agreed to Poor criteria for vendor selection	
	Not coordinating relations with subcontractors and other external parties	
	Improper negotiation planning	
	Insufficient information about the other party	
	Unregulated or undocumented negotiations, or having hasty or negative negotiations	
	Lack of basic legal knowledge on the part of sales and technical teams	
	Inadequate project understanding	
	Lack of project resources	
Contract	The committee evaluating the proposals is not fully aware of the project, or is not impartial Lack of proper negotiation skills Lack of sound negotiation team Absence of binding contract	
	Form of contract does not match with the scope of the project	
	Lack of a fair, robust, and balanced contract	
	Lack of proper communication	

44 See chapter 5 for more details about project phases.

Implementation	No consensus on the implementation approach	
	No detailed agreement on the obligations and responsibilities of each party	
	Lack of interest/documentation of periodic reports and meetings	
	Continuous change requests	
	Heavy modification requests	
	Weak communication between the parties	
	Feeble project management	
	Delay in issuing clearances/approvals	
	Insufficient financing Lack of human resources staff Project plan is not flexible (does not allow for changes) No proper dispute resolution mechanism.	
Post implementation	Lack of clear vision regarding warranties and obligations of both parties during this phase.	
	Lack of agreement on the maintenance and support scope and fees, including updates, upgrades and spare parts. Operation risks: untrained resources, poor documentation ...	
	Not agreeing on the fees for additional services.	

Table 4: Example of Risk Assessment Table

Risk Area	Expected Risks	Extent/ Probability	Comments / Proposed Action
Before Project	Project objectives are ambiguous. Key business requirements are not made clear enough to the bidders.		
	There is doubt regarding the real need for the project.		
	Tender conditions are ambiguous. Tender conditions are burdening/ one- sided. Client terms and conditions do not match the industry standard.		
	The political status within a country or region is unstable and indicative of a problematic situation.		
Scope of Work	Scope of work is not definitively specified. Project deliverables are not clearly set.		
	Probability for modifications and changes		
	System design opened for change requests.		
	A fault in drafting the specifications		
	System acceptance does not match the software at hand.		
	Systems existing with clients are unknown, which may cause integration problems		
	Some of the products are still under development. The technology is new and untried. The technical team is not adequately trained or competent.		

Financial Aspects	Contract value disproportionate to works		
	Payment terms are not linked to clear milestones.		
	One of the contract parties is not financially sound. Insolvency of one of the parties is questionable.		
	No clear list of the items to be delivered. Excessive penalties, performance securities and financial obligations		
	Embargo and difficulties related to currency Payment currency is not stable. The applicable law lies in a different legal family.		
Project Duration	Duration is unrealistic and incommensurate with the scope of work.		
	Duration is too long, to the extent that future events cannot be predicted.		

Legal Aspects	Contract drafting in some places is ambiguous.		
	Appendices and schedules are incomplete. The contract is extremely biased to one party.		
	The capability of one of the parties to fulfil financial responsibilities is doubtful.		
	Some texts depend on unknown or unavailable conditions and information.		
	The type of contract does not match the nature of work.		
	Some definitions are vague or confusing.		
	No proper exit plan No proper dispute escalation and resolution mechanism		
	Lacks in defining responsibilities		
	The delay penalties are excessively high.		
	Contract termination events are unclear.		
	No definition to the "material breach"		
	Poor arbitration clause		
	Schedules are not complete.		
	The overall contract document is not properly arranged.		

Conclusion

As noted in this chapter, the common denominator in all risk areas outlined and discussed, together with the tools utilized to combat the same, is the contract. Hence, it can be stipulated that both the contract (provided coherent and fair) and internal corporate policies can play an extremely significant role in helping parties mitigate the risks involved with software and IT projects. Just as risk areas exist, tools are utilized to avoid those risks; mainly the contract document and the contractual processes.

The approach we call on is based on the premise of the ***"coherent"*** contract, being the general framework and appropriate venue that should contain and accurately record elements for project success. The contract is where the scope of works must be specified; the deliverables detailed; the realistic timeframe for implementation set out; the methodology for sound project management put forth; testing criteria identified; mechanisms for changes and modifications determined; and dispute resolution procedures put into place. This is in addition to any other terms and conditions establishing a ***"fair and balanced"*** contract. It is the contract that grants the parties ample opportunity and time to contemplate – as long as everything will be recorded and documented – the effectiveness of success elements and factors, be they technical, financial, or legal. Of course this assumes that all technicians fulfil their responsibilities to ensure the implementation of technical success elements upon which IT projects are founded; insofar as design, technical specifications, scope of work, availing human and technical resources, proposing a realistic implementation schedule and project management methodologies; and so forth. This should be underlined by clear-cut, professional, and sound contract drafting.

Chapter 3
LEGAL ENVIRONMENT

"Law of Contract - ME Legal System"

Aim of the Chapter

This chapter aims to identify contract basics and principles in various laws and legislations in Middle Eastern countries (Egypt, United Arab Emirates, and Kuwait), explaining the minimum requirements and prerequisites technical and business personnel and others in software and IT fields must be aware of. This is, in fact, one of the most important components of the environment where the IT projects breathe and reanimate. However, this chapter is not legal research in a vacuum. We will view the legal principles "in action" by liking the daily practice to the related legal principals while contracting for IT projects. Additionally, we will outline their provisions and implications on the rights and obligations of contract parties, ensuring theory and practice are given equal weight while emphasizing tips and recommendations that seek to avoid imminent risks.

Background

The contractual document is considered an important topic in the field of legal research and study. Where the term "contract" may seem uncomplicated and straightforward to some, it is far from that, being a complex and far-reaching concern. It rests upon legal theories of a philosophical nature and thus warrants the understanding and awareness of at least the most basic components on the part of IT workers and enthusiasts. This is so that they may be better able to avoid pertinent risks should they wish to utilize the contract as a medium for regulating commercial activities and ensuring project success.

Regardless of the legal definition of a contract, it is undoubtedly a highly significant legal structure in its own right, while also being a great source of risk. Contracts play a vital role in the commercial world and are construed as being a versatile tool available to those engaged in that field, since they can effectively contribute to the success of any commercial activity.[45] It is precisely this reason that we call upon software and IT personnel to familiarize themselves with the theoretical basics of the contractual document, and to afford them the consideration they so aptly deserve.

We would first like to point out that the law, in a general sense, addresses the subject of contracts as being an abstract theory, which contains general terms and conditions that are applicable to various types of contracts. It does so from two perspectives: the first is that a contract is considered one of the sources of commitment and obligation. The second deals with the terms and conditions of specific contracts, which are elaborated upon in detail. As such, even though computer and IT contracts are comprised of unique technical and commercial features, they are still based on and subject to the general theoretical foundation of contract law. Now since the subject pertaining to general contract theory touches upon rather complex and specialized topics, we shall only

---

45 See also next point (Contract Significance).

refer to subjects more intertwined with practicality, while attempting to explain the same in simple and comprehensible terms.[46]

On the other hand, we shed light on numerous legal provisions and basic principles contained in contractual agreements via chapter introductions throughout this volume and the upcoming one. We believe this to be the most practical and effective way in simultaneously facilitating the readers' familiarity with textual basics, provisions, and formulation.

Key point: Civil law in the Middle East (ME) is credited as being the law that has regulated general contract theory and is regarded as being one of the principal laws within the legal system in general, and for civil and commercial transactions in particular. Egypt was the first Arab modern-age state to issue a complete and comprehensive civil code in the Middle East, in 1949, which was greatly influenced by its French counterpart. Accordingly, the Egyptian civil law formed the basis upon which numerous other Arab states construed their own, making it safe to say that with the exception of the kingdom of Saudi Arabia, and Oman, most laws in the Arab world have been significantly impacted by Egyptian civil law (examples include Libya, Iraq, Qatar, Jordan, Sudan, Bahrain, Kuwait, the United Arab Emirates and Yemen). In this book, I will focus on the civil codes of Egypt, UAE and Kuwait, as a specimen of the Middle Eastern legal system.

---

46 Several references (in Arabic language) have been utilized in this section as follows: 1) Hamdy Abdul Rahman, General Commitment Theory – First Book: Voluntary Sources of Commitment – Contract and Unilateral Will, first edition, 1999, Dar Al Nahda. 2) Abdul Fattah Abdul Baqi, Sources of Commitment in Kuwaiti Civil Law, 1981. 3) Mohamed Husam Mahmoud Lotfy, General Commitment Theory – Sources of Commitment – Second Edition –– 2002. 4) Ali Al Baroudy Contracts and Commercial Banking Transactions. 5) Hosni Al Masry Commercial Contracts in Comparative Egyptian and Kuwaiti Law, first edition 1989. Mohamed Husam Mahmoud Lotfy (1999), "Civil Responsibility in the Negotiation Phase- Comparative Study between Egyptian and French Law,", Cairo; Mohamed Abdul Zaher Hussein, "Legal Aspects of the Pre-Contract Stage", 2001.

Contract Significance

The contract plays a substantial and central role in both the general and commercial realms, including the software and IT industries, where the contract can greatly contribute to mitigating associated risks and reducing the rate of failure in software and IT projects.

In elucidating the importance associated with contracts (and indeed one of the most eloquently put statements in this regard), one of the gurus in the field of civil law, Dr Abdul Fattah Abdul Baqi, says: "The contract is a profound system of law in its own right, and plays a formidable role between people in the financial world in particular, being a primary source of rights and obligations. The truth of the matter is that the great majority of obligations and commitments are shaped by the contract, as well as it is the means for amending or transferring any existing obligation".

***Key point*:** It is precisely this significance upon which the notion of this book is based, while asserting the contribution made by the contract in mitigating risks associated with this industry and helping its projects meet with the success they strive for. This has been meticulously detailed throughout the chapters of this book.

The Contract as a Source of Obligation

There exists in law a general theory of "obligations" that dates back to the time of the ancient Romans, to whom credit for its inception should be awarded. In simple terms, obligations constitute a legal theory (or system) that accurately outlines the various rights and obligations arising between two parties: debtor and creditor; vendor and purchaser; lessor and lessee; lender and borrower. As such, this theory holds a significant weight in that it lays the ground upon which overall commitments are based. "Sources of obligation" are matters that generate obligations by one party towards another, as in the contract being a source of obligations for the vendor to deliver goods to the purchaser, and for the purchaser to effect payment for the same. Likewise, the leasing contract constitutes a source of commitment for the lessor to allow the lessee access to the leased unit, and for the lessee to pay due rent and so forth. Accordingly, the contract, in a general sense, is a primary source of obligations[47] – albeit not the sole source – with others including unilateral will, unlawful act (acts causing harm [tort]), enrichment without cause (or acts conferring benefits). Ultimately, the law emerges as a primary source of obligations.

Definition of Contract

Quite simply, the contract is the convergence and coincidence (or agreement, or concord) between two wills to bring about a certain legal effect. The Kuwaiti civil law (article 31) defines the contract[48] as being, "An association of offer and acceptance to bring about an effect that is recognized by law". Accordingly, and drawing upon the aforementioned definition, it becomes apparent that a contract is based on two primary pillars: 1. the existence of a common will between the parties, as exemplified by the association of offer and acceptance – such as the satisfaction and agreement of both parties upon a common issue; and 2. wilfully bringing about an effect that is regulated by law, hence one that is legally binding.

In this respect, we discern the following:

1. The contract warrants the presence of at least two parties, since –in general- no contract exists with only one party or a sole will. In addition, there is nothing to prevent the inclusion of multiple other parties, or that each party constitutes more than one individual.
2. The existence and convergence of two wills and their association by offer and acceptance is insufficient for the creation of a contract, unless both wills are directed towards causing an effect that is recognized by law. In this respect, if you were to

47 This is where the overall importance of the contract emerges, since it is considered a primary source of obligations.

48 Corresponding to Article 125 of the UAE Law, whereas the Egyptian civil law contains no such definition.

invite an acquaintance for dinner and he were to accept your gesture, then both your wills are in agreement. However, these two wills have not converged to cause an effect acknowledged by law, and neither you nor your acquaintance intended to enter a contractual agreement; hence, no contract exists.

3. There does not exist any variation between the following terms: contract, agreement, and contractual agreement, since they all are construed as having the same meaning or definition.
4. The contract is not merely utilized for the creation of a specific commitment or obligation, but also for amending an existing one, or transferring the same from one party to another as well.

Named and Unnamed Contracts

There is no set limit for the various types and categories of contracts, since new contracts emerge frequently, due to the willingness of parties to do so, in a free manner, as long as no malicious or illegitimate activity is intended. However, legal scholars classify some contracts in groups of similar terms and conditions:

Named contracts are the ones given a specific name by the law, and their special provisions have been highlighted, such as sale contract, lease contract, employment contract, company contract, etc.

Unnamed contracts are the ones that have not been designated a name by law and whose special provisions have not been highlighted. These contracts continue to remain "unnamed" even if customarily designated a specific title. We would like to point out here that unnamed contracts – just as all other agreements – are subjected to conditions applicable to other contracts, and thus are not considered to be lacking in legal regulation. Such contracts are subjected to the general regulations of law in addition to any special provisions stipulated by the contracting parties. Examples of named contracts include sale contract, insurance contract, mortgage contract, and contract for work, agency agreement, etc. Most computer and IT contracts are considered unnamed contracts, since the law in Arab nations does not designate them a specific name, nor does it seek to clarify the provisions of the same. This is in spite of the fact that most of these contracts are classified under "contract for work" (*muqawala*, in Arabic), such as the ones governing turnkey projects, software development, and IT outsourcing.

Commercial Contracts

Commercial contracts come under a category of contracts that we ought to examine more closely. Their unique provisions, owing to their direct association with this book, have significant implications on practical life and lasting repercussions on commerce and business. Thus, we can safely proclaim that the set of contracts utilized among vendors and for purposes involving commercial transactions are called commercial contracts and may differentiate from civil contracts by virtue of specific and unique provisions.

This category of commercial contracts contain at least two different types of agreements. One is the original civil contracts that acquire a commercial nature due to the circumstances pertaining to the commercial milieu in which they are utilized. A simple example is a sales contract, a civil contract that is described as a commercial agreement if concluded between merchants. The other type constitutes contracts stipulated by commercial law. These are contracts that are not present in civil law, such as contracts pertaining to transportation, commission agency, commercial mortgages, deposits in public warehouses, commercial agencies and brokerages, and the sale and mortgage of commercial outlets. In addition, a part of this category is titled by the commercial law as "banking operations" such as cash deposit agreements, sukuk (Islamic bonds) deposits, safe-deposit box leasing, security mortgages, banking transmission, letters of credit, letters of guarantee, and current accounts.

What differentiates this set of contracts from civil contracts, in terms of provisions, is manifold:

- **first** is that the parties hereto enjoy a great deal of liberty in forming the contract and forging various forms of the same in accordance with commercial purposes

- **second** is the swiftness by which rights and obligations emanating from a commercial contract may be transferred
- **third** is the ease and quickness of verifying and proving commercial agreements. In origin (for instance) and in accordance with civil law, should legal disposal surpass a specific amount, then the existence of writing proof in verifying its presence or otherwise is not permissible. Moreover, it is not permissible to prove what contradicts the text unless in writing. Yet as far as commercial provisions go, verification has been permitted through all legal means, so the existence of proof verifying the commercial contract is accepted – regardless of its value – and so is the existence of proof, attempting to verify what contradicts the provisions stipulated in the written commercial agreement.
- **fourth** is that the commercial legislator has imposed much despotic regulations insofar as the execution of these contracts. This can be portrayed by the higher interest in the late payment imposed upon commercial matters in comparison to those applied in the case of other civil issues. Another example is that immediate execution process is mandatory by the power of law in verdicts pertaining to commercial provisions. Contrary to civil law, the rule of thumb as far as commercial law (Kuwaiti and Egyptian) is that the joint solidarity between debtors is assumed, and this may only be negated by law or as agreed by the parties. As such, the grace period afforded by civil law is not permissible insofar as the promissory note. Lastly, bankruptcy is considered a harsh commercial resort that removes a merchant defaulting on his debts from commercial life.

***Key Point*:** Here we would like to reiterate that the regulations described for commercial contracts are applicable to computer and IT contracts, should the contract acquire a commercial nature, which is the case more often than not.

Elements of the Contract

The law defines a contract as being "An association involving offer and acceptance on bringing about an effect that is acknowledged by law".[49] Accordingly, this points to the necessity of the contract preserving certain elements and components – without which it cannot be construed – such as *agreement, subject matter, and purpose***.** As per law, the contract comes into force "once acceptance is associated with an offer, once a subject matter is specified upon a legal basis, without violating any requirement of law in some special instances".

As such, contractual elements are as follows:

The **first** element is ***The Agreement:*** This is the assent, mutual agreement, or meeting of minds, which is the first and foremost contractual component. It is the agreement or a co-instance between the two wills and comes across as a result of the following:

a. *The presence of a specific will*, which means a person must be knowledgeable about the matter and must acknowledge the rights and obligations implied, while being legally competent to enter into a contractual agreement. This assent or mutual agreement must be valid, in the sense that it must hold legal competence for both parties to enter into a contractual agreement. Therefore, legal competence is not only a prerequisite; it must also be devoid of any wilful defects such as fraud, deception, coercion, or manipulation. Specifically, the issue of legal competence (especially performance competence) is significant in relation to the business world, since the entitlement of the authorized signatory of any contract must be duly verified. This prevents the agreement being declared null and void due to incompetence or non-entitlement.[50]

b. This will must be looking to *cause a specific legal implication*, for if it seeks to cause an implication that is irrelevant to the law,

---

[49] Article 33 of the Kuwaiti Civil Law; article 129 of the UAE civil law.

[50] There are also some new agreement methods such as shrink-wrap, drop-in-box, and browse-wrap.

or the law does not acknowledge it, then it would be futile and no contract would be feasible.

c. That this will be *expressed to the external world*, in whatever means preferred – orally, in writing, or via any other method that is clearly symptomatic of its intended purpose. This may also be done by adopting any other stance that is indicative of its real intentions – unless a specific expression of the same is required by law in special instances. Should the will be present as described above, it must be associated with the knowledge of the recipient to which it has been directed. Such association should consider the presumption of recipient's knowledge of this will, unless proof exists otherwise.

d. Lastly, it is imperative for the will of both parties to the contract *to be in concord or coincide*. This is achieved in three steps as follows: offer, acceptance and the association between the offer and the acceptance. *The offer* is a proposal put forth by one individual to another for entering into a given contractual agreement, containing all primary components of the desired contractual agreement. The rule of thumb is that the proposal is not binding (i.e. the person suggesting the proposal may retract his offer as long as the proposed party has not yet accepted the same). An exception to this rule (the offer is binding the person who made the offer) is maintained if the offering party specifies a deadline for acceptance. Here this offer will be binding the offering party during the specified deadline and expire at the end of this period. *The acceptance*[51] is accepting the offer made and agreeing to all matters specifically outlined in the proposal – nothing more or nothing less. Should the response to a proposal become deemed to exceed or fall short of the offer, or if it amends the offer in any other way, it shall be construed as a rejection of the same, while entailing a new offer.[52]

***Key Point*:** This is a paramount point to be noted and commands substantial implications in real-life practical situations, especially in

---

51 Acceptance may appear, in practical, in the form of an acceptance letter or letter of intent.

52 Article (43) of the Kuwaiti Civil Law and Article (96) of the Egyptian Civil Law, 140/2 UAE Law.

witnessing that a primary reason for the emergence of disputes between the contracting parties within the IT arena emanates from this specific point (i.e. incongruence of the two wills). What often occurs insofar as systems delivery and software development contracts is that the contracting parties are actually unable to view the final product at the time of contract. They are compelled to settle for merely anticipating that product, owing largely to its intangible nature, so their expectations may diverge extensively.

This is where the role of accurately stating the scope of the contract comes to play, by meticulously describing the system at hand as much as possible while setting in place a mechanism for amending the scope if the need arises.

On the other hand, the offer received in response to a call for tender may be completely incompatible with the required specifications. The question arising here is which conditions would take precedence? Tender conditions may be unrealistic or far-fetched from the prospect of the service provider, or the proposal that was submitted by that service provider,[53] or something else in the middle.

Retracting from the expressed will is possible, on the condition that the same is communicated to the party receiving a counteroffer prior to or at the time of receiving the first offer. In this respect, the law stipulates, "The expression of a will shall have no repercussion if received by a party to which a retraction was directed prior to or at the same time of receipt".[54] In other words, the contract is considered binding upon the two parties if the retraction is not received by the other party prior to its receipt of the first expression of will or at the same time of receipt.

The **second** element of the contract is *the* ***subject matter***, or the *obligations it generates*. The subject matter involves what the parties undertake to do, or refrain from doing. It must comply with three specific conditions. The first is that it must be *feasible;* secondly, it must

53 This response can sometimes take the form of a "compliance matrix", through which the proposing party provides a complete answer to whether he is in compliance with each and every requirement of the project.

54 Article (94) of the Egyptian civil law; Article (136) onwards of the UAE Law.

be *defined, or capable of being defined;* and third, it must be *legitimate* and not in conflict with public order or decency.

***Key Point*:** It becomes apparent that the subject matter element constitutes an extreme importance to contract formation, particularly the second aforementioned condition (*being defined, or capable of being defined*). This is because the contracting parties in this field often agree on an intangible subject matter or one that is not accurately defined, one that only exists in the expectations of each. Surely this gives rise to the issue of the contract subject matter, or the extent of accurately detailing the subject of the agreement regarding IT contracts. In other words, it is the software requiring development or the IT system to be constructed explicitly defined in such a manner that avoids the rise of future disputes between the parties. Even though the subject matter may be futuristic,[55] the contract may be deemed null and void unless "the subject matter is defined so as to rule out complete ignorance".[56] In this respect, "complete ignorance" refers here – and as explained by Islamic Sharia scholars – to an ignorance that is likely to lead to conflict.[57] From a practical and realistic perspective, the subject matter of computer and IT contracts is the "scope of contract" and is, in my humble opinion, the most crucial article stipulated thereof, owing to it constantly being a source of dispute. Conflicts usually arise due to the lack of accuracy and detail in describing the subject matter (or scope), as often explained throughout this book.

The **third** contractual element is ***the purpose*** of the agreement, or simply the end both parties seek to achieve as a result of the commitment and obligations made. For instance, a merchant would undertake to transfer the ownership of sold goods to the purchaser, provided he receives payment for the same, since the price of goods for him constitutes the purpose of the contract. Similarly, the purchaser commits to affecting the price payment on condition of acquiring the sold goods, the goods being his purpose of the contract. While applying the above to software and IT contracts, we observe that from the client's perspective, the services rendered or deliverables achieved, or the "new IT system"

55 Article (37) of the Kuwaiti civil law.

56 Article (171/1) of the Kuwaiti civil law.

57 Abdul Baqi, Op.Cite, 414.

received all are regarded as being the purpose of the contract. For the supplier, the purpose is defined as being the material gain received upon rendering his expertise, together with increasing his revenues and boosting his commercial stature.

A clear distinction must be made between "the purpose" and the "subject matter" of the contract. The purpose must answer why has the commitment been made? Whereas the subject matter answers the question of what commitments were being made. Accordingly, the purpose is considered the cornerstone, without which a contract may not be created, so the law stipulates that a contract shall be declared null and void, "Should there be no purpose for the undertaken commitment, or should the purpose be in conflict with public order and decency, or should it be based upon any other illegitimate purpose".[58] An example of nullifying the contract due to the absence of purpose is asking whether the purchaser should commit to paying for something non-existent; whereas an example of voiding the agreement due to its illegitimacy is when one individual, for example, purchases a car from another while paying him for it in narcotics, or by committing any other crime.

Can Silence be Construed as an Expression of Will?

Silence may not be considered an offer or an expression of offer, since it must include a description of the transaction and its terms and conditions, which cannot be accomplished by silence. A silence that is not accompanied by circumstances that validate its significance is also not an expression of acceptance. For instance, should a paper or magazine owner dispatch an issue to an individual for the purpose of soliciting his subscription, then that person's silence or refrain from responding cannot be considered an acceptance of subscription – even if advised to the contrary by the newspaper or magazine publisher.

One type of silence, referred to as "*associated silence*", or one that is associated with circumstances deeming it an expression of approval,

58 Article (136) of the Egyptian law; article (207) of the Emirati law.

is considered by law as proof for satisfaction and acceptance,[59] on condition that, "Silence shall be construed as acceptance should there be previous transaction between the parties, and should the acceptance be associated with that transaction or if the offer resulted in pure benefit to whom the offer was directed". As such, the law has set forth several examples of where such associated silence is considered an acceptance:

a. The existence of previous dealings between parties, such as a wholesale vendor who has grown accustomed to dispatching a certain volume of goods to a retailer who, in turn, has also become accustomed to rejecting the unfavourable and accepting what he favours. Should he become silent for a reasonable period following a specific transaction, that silence shall be construed as acceptance.
b. The purchaser actually receiving the purchased goods, whereby should the seller send him an invoice for the same – containing specific terms and conditions – and where the purchase receives the invoice and maintains his silence for a reasonable period, this too shall be construed as an acceptance of the terms of the invoice.
c. Silence is also considered an acceptance should it emanate in response to an offer or proposal containing some sort of benefits or return to whom the offer was directed. This may be illustrated by an example of one individual sending a letter to another offering to settle a debt owed to a third party. Should the recipient remain silent, his silence shall be considered an acceptance of the offer. As such, the sender may not refute his commitment on the basis that the recipient failed to respond, since silence here is considered an acceptance of a valid proposal.

Is it Permissible to Retract from the Contract after Associating the Offer with the Acceptance?

The law is clear-cut when it comes to an acceptance being associated with an offer, stipulating that the contract becomes in full force and

---

59 Article (44/)1 of the Kuwaiti law; article (98/ 2) of the Egyptian law; article (135) of UAE law.

thus impossible to retract. According to Article 47 of the Kuwaiti civil law,[60] "Should acceptance become associated with an offer, then the contract becomes binding to the parties hereto, with neither party being entitled to decline their commitment, unless otherwise agreed or warranted by law or custom". Article 267 of UAE law provides, "If the contract is valid and binding, it shall not be permissible for either of the contracting parties to resile from it, nor to vary or rescind it, save by mutual consent or an order of the court or under a provision of the law". Accordingly, once the parties have signed the agreement, neither may be entitled to retract, unless through the means stipulated by the same contract or by virtue of law.

***Key Point*:** For this reason, we caution the executives as well as authorized signatories that contract signature marks the conclusion of the negotiation phase, and the agreement, then becomes effective with no possibility of retracting from contract terms and conditions, unless as stipulated by the contractual agreement and as specified by law or applicable custom.[61]

Letter of Intent

Within the context of commercial transactions, we often witness parties resorting to signing various[62] legal documents prior to actual contract signature. These documents are referred to as "letters of intent" or "memorandum of understanding", with the former being one form of pre-contract documents" generally concluded by the parties during the negotiation phase or in the pre-signature phase of the final contract. It is a common expression and not a legal one. In general, such documents usually manifest the desire of the parties (or one party) to enter into a contractual agreement for a specific purpose, and so addressing the

---

60 Responding to Article (147/1) of the Egyptian law.

61 In this respect, and according to the British, "In business, as in opera, it is not over until it 'sings'". It is fine within reason to negotiate changes in a written contract up until the moment you sign it.

62 See Dr. Mohamed Husam Mahmoud Lotfy "Civil Responsibility in the Negotiation Phase", Op, Cite. Mohamed Abdul Zaher Hussein, "Legal Aspects for Pre-Contract Stage", Op Cite, page 2.

other party by virtue of one of these documents constitutes a common practice in the IT world. Often one party will approach the other with an offer pertaining to the purchase of an IT system (whether a turnkey system, a software package, a device or number of devices, etc.). Should the proposal meet the requirements of the purchaser, and prior to both parties instigating negotiations associated with the project details, or prior to the formulation of the final contract, they sign a memorandum containing their mutual desire to enter into an agreement, while stipulating some preliminary terms and conditions. The purchase may dispatch an official letter advising his acceptance of the proposal, and his intention to enter into a contractual agreement on the basis of what is stipulated in the received offer. In this respect, letters of intent raise several problems, primarily due to their ambiguity (as they are often formulated by non-legal personnel), or because of containing patchy agreements.

What Is the Legal Value of These Documents?

In responding to this question, we would like to point to article 95 of the Egyptian civil law, which states, "Should the parties agree on all fundamental contract issues, and maintain detailed issues upon which they intend on agreeing on a later date – unless otherwise they agree that the contract will not be concluded if the parties could not agree on such detailed issues – then the contract shall be considered to be in force. Should a dispute arise from the subjects to be discussed by the parties later, the court shall adjudicate on the same in accordance with the nature of the transaction, the law, customs, and justice". With the exact meaning and almost same language, article 52 of the Kuwaiti civil law stipulates, "Should the parties agree on the most fundamental contractual components, and suspend only secondary issues in the hopes to agree on the same later, then this shall not prevent the contract coming into force. Should the parties fail to agree on the adjourned secondary matters, the judge shall proceed to resolve the dispute in accordance with the nature of the transaction, the prevailing custom and judicial requirements".

From the previous provisions, we note the following:

1. The legislator, in the case of both parties failing to agree on the secondary matters, was faced with two options: either consider the contract non-existent, or, should any dispute arise regarding the secondary matters, consider the agreement in effect pending adjudication by a judge. We note that the legislator adopted the latter option.
2. As a general rule of thumb, and for the contract to be deemed effective, the parties must agree to the fundamentals of the contract. As for secondary details, these are not pivotal for construing a contractual agreement, whereby both parties may agree to decide on the same on a later date. This too does not undermine the contract validity, since a judge undertakes to resolve any disputes arising in this regard.
3. The aforementioned rule is not an absolute, as contract terms and conditions or surrounding circumstances should indicate the intent of the parties to defer contract signature until both fundamental and secondary issues have been agreed. In such a case, this intention must be revered in that the contract is not declared valid until the moment when both parties concur on all agreement details, fundamental and secondary.
4. Differentiating between fundamental and secondary details can often be easily accomplished in most instances. The following, for instance, are fundamental to IT contracts: system description, scope of contract, prices, contract duration, and acceptance, services, payment terms, and payment method.
5. In applying the previous rules, for instance, on the text appearing in a software-development contract that parties – upon completion of the development process and production of the final product – shall sign a joint marketing agreement for the developed software. Such provision holds no legal weight unless the parties specify the fundamental components of the intended joint marketing operation. This incorporates the regional scope of marketing, the rights and commissions of each party and the primary obligations, etc. Likewise, a contract for the delivery of a comprehensive IT system that stipulates a supplier's commitment to maintaining and supporting the system has no bearing, unless the fundamental details of the same (scope of maintenance and support, fees, etc.) are agreed upon.

6. The above rules are also applicable to the letter of intent (LOI), which is in fact a form of contractual agreement since it involves a mutual desire to accomplish a certain objective. The legal value of the LOI depends to a great extent on its contents (i.e. its incorporation of the fundamental terms and components of the primary interaction). So in the application of the aforementioned, the LOI commands a sizeable legal value, and the contract comes into force and becomes obligatory to both parties, even if they continue to differ on secondary details. This is on condition that the parties (or either party) have not explicitly conditioned the contract to become valid only after settling other detailed issues, or pending "final contract signature", or any other reservation.
7. We would also like to touch upon what we had mentioned earlier regarding acceptance. Should the LOI state client acceptance of the submitted proposal from the supplier without reservation of any kind, this shall be construed as an acceptance of the offer, and the contractual agreement would take effect. However, should the LOI contain some reservations or conditions, or defer the final approval on another issue, no acceptance exists and it holds no legal value.

Accordingly, I advise the relevant parties not to resort to LOIs in the absolute sense, and to carefully read their contents in order to ascertain their legal weight and value, prior to burdening themselves with baseless legal or financial obligations. Indeed, many such documents drafted in the English language contain the phrase *subject to contract*, implying the parties are still in the negotiation phase and that agreements reached thus far are not binding until the final contract has been signed.

Civil Responsibility in the Negotiation Phase

The negotiation phase taking place prior to contract signature is quite important in that it directly impacts the contents, extends the rights and obligations of the parties, and because it may constitute a source of civil responsibility. This means the violating party may be held accountable should it transgress a specific legal obligation. Yet it is often overlooked and not treated with the care and attention it rightfully deserves.

The negotiating parties must be aware of two fundamental issues to avoid civil responsibility during the pre-contract phase:

One must completely refrain from any deceptive, misleading, fraudulent, and misrepresenting action during this phase, as this implies civil responsibility and may cause the contract to be declared null and void. In this respect, article 151 of the Kuwaiti civil law states, "A party shall be entitled to request voiding the contractual agreement should it be able to prove that its acceptance was obtained via deception, and that it would not have otherwise consented, notwithstanding articles 153 and 154".

Article 125 of the Egyptian civil law stipulates, "The contract may be voided by reason of deception, should deception behaviour committed by one of the parties or its representatives be so flagrant to the extent that the second party would not have concluded the contract".

Article 187 of the Emirati law states, "If one of the contracting parties makes a misrepresentation to the other and it transpires that the contract was concluded by a gross cheat, the person so misled may cancel the contract".

Second numerous other obligations bind the contracting parties during the negotiation phase, the violation of which results in holding the breaching party accountable. These obligations can be listed as follows[63]:

- Commitment to notify: the parties must present true and valid information pertaining to the deal at hand.
- Commitment to enquire: the parties must seek to gain complete and comprehensive knowledge of the circumstances and conditions surrounding the deal at hand.
- Commitment to honesty: the parties must refrain from submitting false or obsolete information or data.

---

63 Husam Lofty, Op, Cite.

- Commitment to cooperation: the parties must be willing to assist one another in culminating the negotiation phase to a logical end, whether the contract leads to signature or otherwise.
- Commitment to reasonableness and genuineness: the parties must be prepared to lead flexible discussions and to be open for additional consideration and reflection.
- Commitment to confidentiality: the parties must refrain from disclosing any confidential or propriety information.
- Commitment to respecting customs and traditions: the parties must revere and observe professional customs and other local or national considerations pertaining to the deal at hand.

***Key Point*:** In conclusion and as previously reiterated, the infringement of any of the aforementioned duties and obligations may constitute grounds for contract nullification, as well as a source of civil responsibility. This is because these commitments, or part thereof, embody faults that are eligible for compensation and damages.

Commercial Customs in Software and IT Contracts

Commercial customs play a significant role in the world of business and commerce, equating legislation insofar as commercial matters, especially since they are given priority of implementation before a judge, and the application of a legal authoritative or complimentary text pertaining to civil matters.

A custom is defined as being a specific behaviour or action to which individuals have become accustomed, and which is considered by them to be binding. It may be a complimentary factor that fills a certain void or one that remedies an intentional or unintentional ambiguity. Customs are even more significant regarding computer and IT contracts, due to the unique nature and characteristics of this particular industry. By way of example, the following are among the most prevalent customs in the field:

1. Software, by nature, is prone to errors and defects, and the presence of these is not uncommon and does not constitute a

violation. Indeed, an English court has adjudicated the same through a ruling issued by the Court of Appeals in 1995. It was held that "Software is not a commodity which is delivered once, only once, and once and for all, but one which will necessarily be accompanied by a degree of testing and modification".[64] It would not be a breach[65] of contract to deliver software in the first instance with a defect in it.

2. Another example is the cooperation and coordination between the supplier and the client, upon which the success of IT projects, is founded. In a famous case witnessed by the British courts, the court blamed the client for failing to demonstrate sufficient cooperation with the supplier, and the judge expressed concern about the unprofessional and uncooperative conduct of the client, stating clearly that, "It is understood in both the legal and IT worlds that the installation of an IT system requires close and extensive cooperation on the part of those involved, which necessitates client's acceptance of reasonable solutions to any of the technical issues that may arise throughout the project".[66] He went on to assert that software delivery contracts implicitly require the customer to:
   i. communicate clearly any special needs to the supplier
   ii. take reasonable steps to ensure the supplier understands those needs

And the supplier communicates to the purchaser:

i. whether those precise needs can be met, and if so, how they can be met. If they cannot be precisely met, the appropriate options should be set by the supplier.
ii. to take reasonable measures to ensure that the client has been adequately trained to operate the new system

---

64 Saphina computing v Allied Collection Agencies Litd, referred to in the below source.

65 Ian J Lloyd Information Technology Law, Forth Edition, (2011), England: Oxford University Press, 586.

66 Diane Rowland, Op, Cite, page 464.

iii. to work with the client jointly to resolve any issues that, as the judge put it, "will almost certainly occur".[67]

3. Another customary rule that is acknowledged in the area of turnkey system delivery is that: the system (upon completion of acceptance tests and following warranty) shall be in the possession of the client and under his responsibility, and the supplier would not be accountable for any risks or hazards arising from the system (unless within the scope of the maintenance contract).
4. Another custom relates to data responsibility throughout the project, since databases always fall under the responsibility of the client. In fact, it may be impermissible for the supplier, during system implementation, to approach or view databases due to the confidentiality and propriety nature of the information they contain.
5. We also note that customary practices command numerous applications in law, such as the role played by custom in interpreting any ambiguous texts in the contract. In this regard, article 265 of the Emirati law states that contract interpretation is founded upon "the nature of the transaction and the trust and integrity existing between the contracting parties in accordance with customary practices".
4. Customs also play a role in determining what is considered "contract appurtenant", since article 148 of the Egyptian law asserts that in general, any contract is not merely limited to its expressed contents but also includes "as required by law, custom, and justice." In the same context, article 246/2 of the UAE law provides: "The contract shall not be restricted to an obligation upon the contracting parties to do that is [expressly] contained in it, but shall also embrace that is appurtenant to it by virtue of the law, custom, and the nature of the transaction".

[67] Ibid.

Contract Interpretation

It is understood that contractual contents must express a joint will of both parties in a clear and concise manner. Should this be the case, there exists no need for interpretation, and a judge is obligated to consider the explicit meaning. Article 193/1 of the Kuwaiti civil law provides, "Should the contract be formulated in a clear and comprehensible language, then there is no need to interpret its terms in order to determine the will of the parties thereto".

However, if this is not the case, and the mutual will of the parties appears to be rather ambiguous, this paves the way for interpretations into their true intent. Article 193/2 of the Kuwaiti civil law stipulates: "The joint intent of the contracting parties must be deducted by means of the overall contract conditions and circumstances, and should not merely be limited to contract phrases or wording, while being guided by the nature of the transaction, current customary practice, goodwill, and honourable dealings". Article 265 of the Emirati law and Article 150 of the Egyptian law stipulate the same.

If the judge finds no difficulty in interpreting the ambiguity of the contract wording, then he should proceed and apply his own interpretation on the grounds of the rules and guides imposed by the legislator in the previous article. Otherwise, he should inure the interpretation to the benefit of the debtor. Article 194, paragraph one of the Kuwaiti civil law states, "Should it not be possible to resolve the ambiguity of the contract, insofar as the true intent of the parties thereto, and the doubt still remains, then the benefit of the doubt shall be given to the party prone to the greatest damage by the application of the text". Paragraph two of the same article goes on to state, "Specifically, the benefit of the doubt shall be with the debtor should the condition burden him with a commitment", with similar provisions found in Article 266 of the Emirati law and Article 151/1 of the Egyptian law.

Key Point: To recap, the ambiguity of contractual texts opens the door for interpretation on the part of a judge, in case a dispute arises, and more so if the contractual agreement lacks these texts altogether. Note that the matter may reach a completely different outcome contrary to the one intended by the parties, such as in the case the judge is unable to clarify any ambiguity or if both parties continue to firmly hold their ground. Here the judge will rule in favour of the indebted part, even if this is unintended by both. This is precisely why parties and their respective consultants/advisors must ensure that contractual agreements are formulated in a clear and concise language, and that all agreed terms and conditions are outlined and essential details are listed.

Contractual Contents

As depicted by Article 195 of the Kuwaiti civil law: "A contract is not merely limited to legal provisions, but also includes requirements, in accordance with the customary practice and matters of justice, while paying heed to the nature of the transaction, goodwill, and honourable dealing". Article 148 of the Egyptian code and 246/2 of the UAE code adopt the same concept. As such, contractual contents include the following provisions:

- provisions contained in contract terms, whether explicit or implicit
- provisions pertaining to commercial custom prevalent at the place of contract
- legal provisions that apply to the contractual agreement, regardless of whether they emanate from legislation or from customary practice
- provisions that are considered contract requirements, such as provisions warranted by its nature and the purpose that it targets, in accordance with law, custom, and justice while acting in goodwill

***Key point*:** For that, contractors in the IT industry must be careful when pricing the scope of the project. They may find themselves responsible for providing items that are not listed in the contract. Based on the above concept, any equipment, materials, system design, software, interfaces, integration requirements, and the like, which is necessary for the completion of the project and to meet the system performance in accordance with the agreed specifications, shall be provided by the contractor at no additional cost.

Binding Force of Contract

Should the contract come into effect and is deemed clearly and concisely formulated, it then acquires a legally binding force and is not subjected to unilateral amendment or breach by either party. As stipulated by article 267 of the UAE code: "If the contract is valid and binding, it shall not be permissible for either of the contracting parties to resile from it, nor to vary or rescind it, save by mutual consent or an order of the court, or under a provision of the law". In the same context, article 196 of the Kuwaiti and 147/1 Egyptian civil codes provide, "Contract clauses is the law of the parties, and as such, neither party shall be entitled to unilaterally breach or amend its provisions, unless as permitted by the agreement or by the law".

***Key Point*:** As such, the contract is a sturdy tool. Being well organized and structured enough, it plays a significant role in the business arena. The contract system should not be taken lightly, and (except in the general exceptional events) neither party may assume it can evade carrying out what has been agreed upon with the other party.[68]

Contractual Liability

This is one of those salient topics, both in the contract theory and between parties in the real life. It refers to the penalty imposed by the law in the event that a party breaches one or more of its contractual obligations. The contractual liability (i.e. breach of contract) is founded on three conditions:

Contractual fault is a fault occurs if a party fails to perform any of its contractual obligations; *damage i*ncurre*d* by the other party resulting from the contractual fault; and finally, the *causal rapport* (causation) between the fault and the damage occurred.

68 See (contract as source of obligation) early in this chapter.

This means that such a liability fails to exist if none of the parties commits any fault, or if a party commits fault but no damage occurs as a result, or if a party does indeed commit a fault and damage is incurred, yet no causation exists between the two.

Taking This Issue Further

Fault

Fault occurs where, without any lawful excuse, a party: a) fails (or refuses) to perform an obligation, partially or entirely; b) delays in performing the obligation; and c) performs his obligation defectively, in the sense of failing to match the quality or specification required by the contract.

The law does not discern a difference between fraud, grievous fault, or minimal fault, in spite of the differing nature of each. As such, the defaulting party is considered liable for the committed fault, whether it may be fraud, grievous, or minimal fault.

Moreover, the breaching party is not relieved of its responsibility unless it is proven that the delay or lack of execution was due to an external reason. This is asserted by article 386 of the Emirati civil law, which states, "Should it become impossible for a party to carry out an obligation, then he shall be made to compensate the other party for this failure, unless it is proven that the lack of implementation occurred due to an external reason over which there is no control. The same shall apply in case of delayed implementation". This corresponds to article 215 of the Egyptian law and Article 293 of Kuwaiti law.

We also note that in some instances, the defaulting party may be responsible for faults committed by another party, whereby the original contractor may be held accountable for a fault committed by the subcontractor. This is in accordance with article 661 of the Egyptian civil law, article 890 of the Emirati law, and article 681 of the Kuwaiti law.

Damage

Should there be no damage, then no liability exists. So if the aggrieved party is unable to prove that the fault committed by the other party has caused any damage, then the contractual liability ceases to be.

Damage may be classified into two categories, material and moral. Material damage comes in three forms: *actual* damage, which has indeed occurred; *future* damage, which has not yet occurred but would inevitably occur in the future; and *potential* damage, which may or may not occur, and is thus not compensated until it actually materializes.

Causation

This designates that the damage is a *"direct result"* of the fault, and that both are linked by a causal relationship.

If fault and damage are proved to have occurred in the contractual relationship, then the causal relationship between them is assumed, in the sense that the aggrieved party is not obliged to prove it. Accordingly, the burden of negating the existence of a causal relationship between the fault and damage lies upon the defaulting party.

Compensation (Damages)

Compensation is the most common remedy for breach of contract, and seeks to indemnify the aggrieved party for losses, which it suffered, and any gain of which it was deprived. As a general rule, if it appears impossible for the obligor to give specific performance of an obligation, he will be ordered to pay compensation to the other party for non-performance (or delay) of his obligation, unless it is proved that the impossibility of performance arose out of external cause in which (the obligor) played no part (386 UAE, 215 Egypt, 293 Kuwait). Egyptian and Kuwaiti laws added: provided that the suffered losses or the gain deprived is a normal result of the non-performance or delay in performance. It will be deemed so if the other party was not able to avoid it after exerting reasonable effort (221/1 Egypt-300/2 Kuwait).

The rule of thumb is that compensation only encompasses "direct" damage that has occurred. This is provided that such damages are "anticipated" at the time of contract, unless the aggrieved party is able to prove that the defaulting party has committed an act of fraud or grievous fault, wherein such case the defaulting party is held accountable for direct damage, whether anticipated or otherwise (221/2 Egypt, 300/3 Kuwait).

The extent of damage must be considered as the main criteria to assess the due compensation, not the gravity of fault committed (i.e. if the harm is grievous compared to the fault, and then the harm will be considered in the assessment of the compensation, not the fault). This is understood because the underlying idea is to remedy the harm suffered by the aggrieved party.

Presumably, the time of damage assessment is the time when the damage occurred (389 UAE). However, for reasons of practicality, in the Egyptian judicial system, compensation is estimated at the time of which adjudication is passed. Compensation is only due for actual damage and not for potential damage unless they are deemed to have actually occurred, or are bound to occur in future.

Compensation is granted for both material and moral damages. The judge is authorized to reduce the amount of compensation or even not to adjudicate any if the other party participated in the occurrence of damage or increased it (216 Egypt, 294 Kuwait, 290 UAE).

Compensation shall not be due if a proper notice has not been given, unless there is a contrary provision in the law or in the contract (387 UAE, 218 Egypt, 279 Kuwait). Parties can agree in the contract on the compensation due to either of them in case of breach of any of them to his obligations, as shown in the consensual compensation paragraph below.

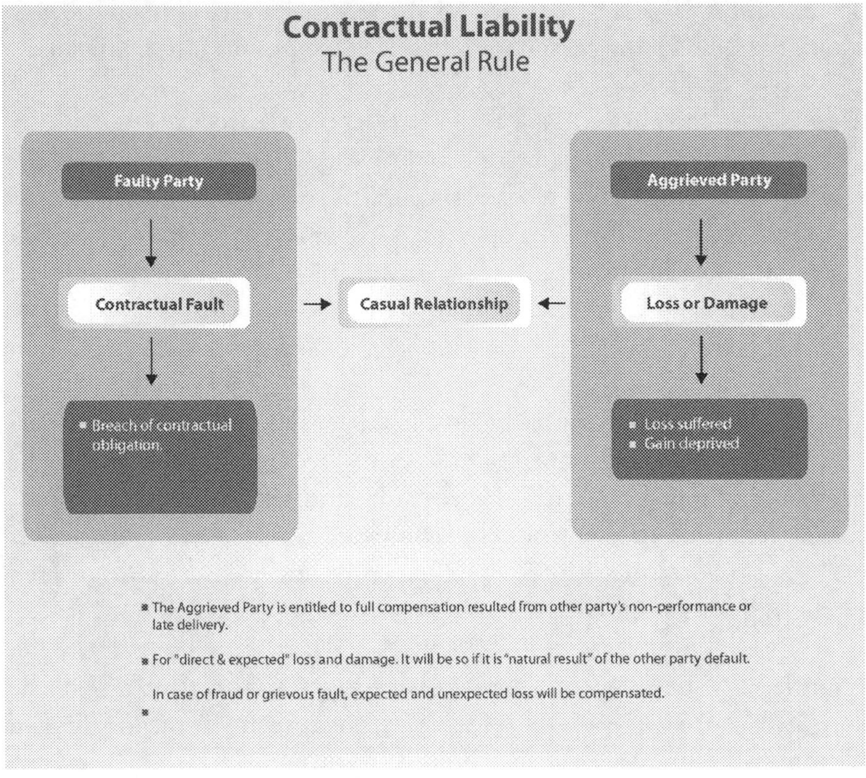

Figure 1: Contractual Liability

Modifying the Liability Rules

- Amending liability regulations refers to toughening, limiting, or relieving a party from liability at a date preceding the occurrence of damage, whereas should the same transpire following the damage, then it is categorized under reconciliation or settlement of contracts.
- It is possible to *toughen* the liability of the defaulting party (such as to obligate him to compensate the other party for direct and indirect damage, or to bear the incident of force majeure and sudden events and its consequences. To *limit* that liability means to restrict or limit the extend of liability (to put a maximum cap

of one party liability), or to agree upon *excluding* (exemption) a party from any liability for his contractual breach.

- Laws exclude any such relief from liability in cases where damage afflicts an individual in his body, life, or morals. Death and bodily injury cannot be excluded.
- It is possible to relieve the defaulting party from any liability arising from non-performance of his contractual commitments, except arising from fraudulent behaviour or blatant error. However, it is allowed to exclude his liability arising out of fraudulent behaviour or gross fault on the part of individuals employed by him in carrying out his obligations (217/2 Egypt, 296 Kuwait).
- In conclusion, limiting or excluding the defaulting party's liability is legally permissible, with some exceptions, such as death, bodily injury, fraudulent behaviour, and/or gross error. This is frequently represented in software and IT contracts by virtue of "limits of liability". The general principles in the ME legal system upon which this clause may be formulated is shown in Figure 2.

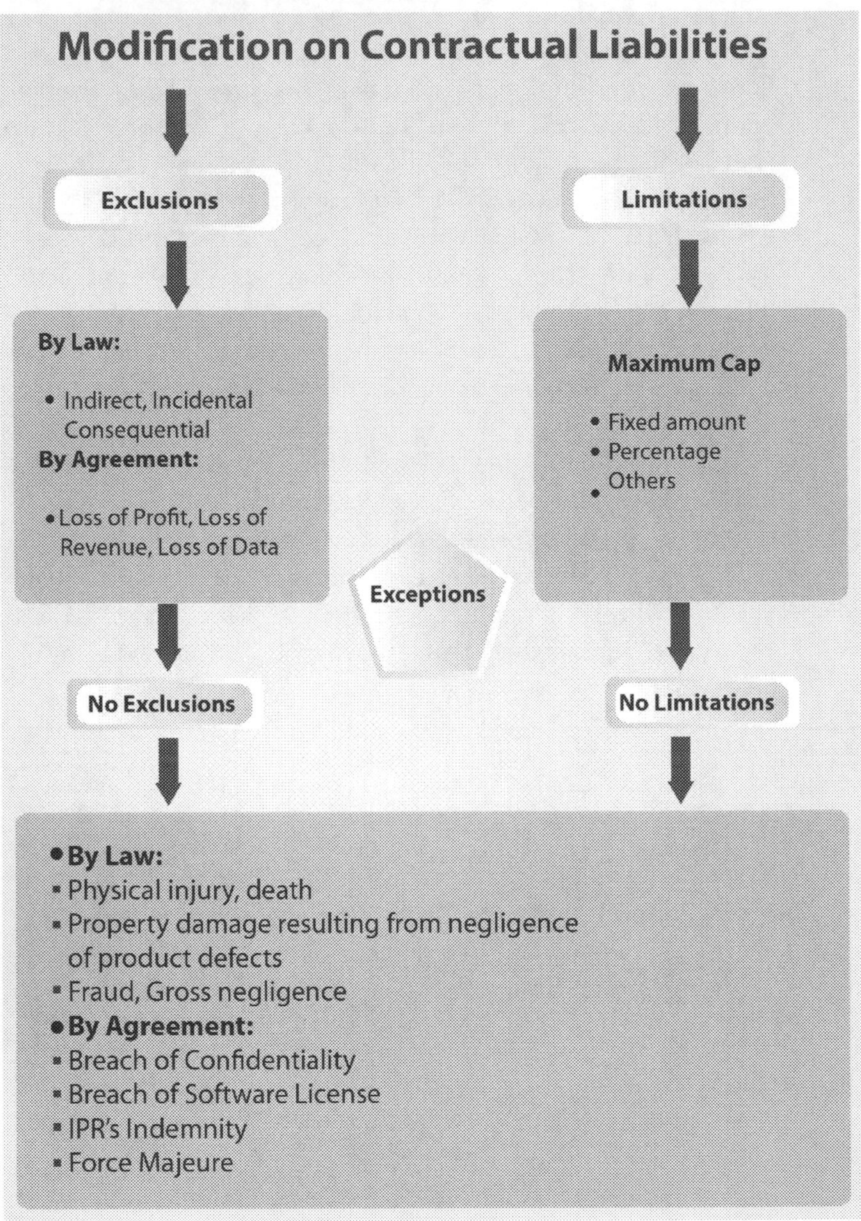

Figure 2: Modification on Contractual Liabilities

Consensual Compensation (Penalty Clause)

According to Middle Eastern laws (Egypt, UAE, Kuwait, and Qatar), it is possible for the contracting parties to agree beforehand on the compensation due to either of them as a result of the damage resulting from breaching part or all of contractual obligations or delay in implementation. This is known as the "penalty clause" and is a principle that was originally derived from Islamic Sharia. The Egyptian law has regulated this principle through article 223, which states, "The parties shall be entitled to agree in advance upon a compensation value to be set forth in the contractual agreement or in a subsequent agreement, taking in consideration articles 215–220".

Article 224/1 and 2 of the same law stipulates that, "Consensual compensation shall not be due should one party be able to prove that no damage has been incurred by the other party. A judge shall have the right to decrease the compensation value if a party proves that the estimated compensation was greatly exaggerated, or that the original obligation was partly executed. Any agreement found to be in conflict with the provisions of the two aforementioned paragraphs shall be considered null and void".

Almost the same wording exists in article 303 of Kuwaiti law. The Emirati law is slightly different in this point. Article 390 provides: "The parties shall be entitled to fix the compensation value in advance, by making a provision therefore, in the contract or in a subsequent agreement subject to the provisions of law, and a judge may – in all cases upon the request of one of the parties – shall have the right to vary such agreement so as to ensure that the estimated value is commensurate with the damage incurred. Any agreement contradicting the above shall be deemed null and void".

Taking This Issue Further

Consensual compensation is a fixed sum that can be agreed upon between the contracting parties in advance, and imposed upon breach or violation of any contractual obligation, or delay in carrying out the same. It may also be enforced in case of partial non-compliance, such as failing to achieve the agreed upon service level or similar, and is often a specific charge computed per day or week of delay after the original deadline for implementation and delivery. A maximum ceiling for the compensation is also specified.

Should the compensation value not be estimated in the contract (such as through a penalty clause), then it is subject to a judge's discretion to estimate the appropriate amount that can remedy the damage – as equivalent to the damage that may usually be anticipated at the time of contract (article 221/1 of the Egyptian law, or that which has indeed been incurred [Article 389 of the Emirati law]).

The advantage of the penalty clause becomes overt insofar as in the area of proof, for once a fault occurs by a party, it is declared that the damage is presumptive. Thus, the burden of proof lies upon the defaulting party that commits the fault to verify that damage was not incurred or that it had indeed occurred, but less than what is estimated in the contract or happened because of force majeure.

We note that the penalty clause commands a threatening tone in that it aims, in part, to deter the defaulting part from neglecting its obligations.

Concerning the judicial control on the parties' agreement: the judge holds the jurisdiction for amending the agreed compensation (by reducing it in the Egyptian law [224/2] and the Kuwaiti law [303]) if the debtor proves that the estimation of the consensual compensation was greatly exaggerated or the original obligation has been partially executed. Moreover, the judge has the power to reject the application of the agreed consensual compensation if the debtor proves the other party incurred no harm. Any agreement between parties contrary to this will be invalid. If the damage exceeds the agreed compensation, the judge has no power to increase the compensation unless the party who inures harm is able to prove that the debtor has committed an act of fraud of gross fault (225 Egypt). Under the UAE law, the judge has a wider authority to "make the compensation equal the loss, also any agreement to the contrary shall be void" (390/2). This is contrary to what is adopted by common-law countries where the judge does not enjoy that authority. As such, caution must be exercised as to the applicable law in effect.

We observe here that this reflects a significant and underlying principle of Islamic Sharia, that being justice. In fact, Arab laws consider any agreement between the parties found to be in contradiction to this as being invalid. Accordingly, the judge may reduce the agreed compensation amount to the sum deemed appropriate, should a party prove that the other party did not in fact suffer any losses, or that losses were less than stated, or that the original commitment was fulfilled entirely or partially.

Liquidated Damages

This type of compensation discussed above is familiar in common-law countries under the title "liquidated damages" and is considered an exception to the general rule of compensation being commensurate to the actual damage occurred due to non-performance or incomplete or delayed implementation. Liquidated damages are permissible on the condition that they must reflect a "genuine pre-estimate of loss". The clause is applied in this case, regardless of the other party incurring any damage or otherwise, which, as explained above, is contrary to the principle adopted by the law in most of the Arab-Pan Region, where amending the agreed compensation is permitted so that it is commensurate with the actual damage, while noting the slight discrepancy between the Egyptian/Kuwaiti and Emirati laws.

Taking This Issue Further

In this regard, we would like to accentuate the following observations:

Accepting and employing this clause is considered an exception to the general principles of law in nations adopting the common-law legal system, which only considers compensation arising out of "actual loss" suffered by the aggrieved party, due to the other party's failure to carry out its contractual obligations or its delay of the same. This is provided that a "genuine pre-estimate of the loss" that the aggrieved party may suffer is reflected, meaning that the estimate must not imply the imposition of a penalty, threat, or pressure placed upon the other party. If this condition is fulfilled, the provision would come into effect, even if the party does not suffer an actual loss. If not, the courts will not enforce the liquidated damages clause because it is a "penalty" or it has been used by one party as a means of pressure or oppression on the other.[69]

This principle secures the interest of both parties. The contractor would be made aware in advance and upon contract signature of the ceiling of compensation to which he would be obligated, should he fail to carry out – or delay – his contractual obligations. Accordingly, he would be able to estimate all risks pertaining to the project at hand. The employer would be exempted from the burden of proving the actual loss occurred, since this provision relieves him of so doing.

As we said, the agreed compensation is of a compensatory nature and is not construed as a form of penalty, meaning the purpose of the same is to compensate the aggrieved party for damage incurred due to an error committed by the defaulting party. As previously explained, it must reflect, upon contract signature, the value of compensation due to the aggrieved party, and nothing more. If it becomes apparent that the agreed compensation implies a penalty or penalization, then it shall not be enforceable. Accordingly, should the offending party wish to evade affecting the agreed compensation, it should simply prove that the compensation does in fact imply penalization.

As far as liquidated damage in common-law countries is concerned, it is implemented as is, even if no damage arises from contractual violation. Moreover, the agreed amount may not be amended and the court has no authority in this regard, provided that the compensation value reflects a genuine estimation of such compensation.

In summary; the laws of Middle East (ME) nations that have adopted the Egyptian model, follow the principle of liquidated damages as well. However,

---

69 Robert Bond, Op, Cite, 120.

they do not differentiate between whether the agreed amount is a genuine estimation to the compensation or if it constitutes penalization. Perhaps the reason for this is that these laws allow for amending the agreement so that it is partially commensurate with the actual loss suffered by the aggrieved party.[70]

End of Contract (Contract Dissolution)

According to the general principal in the ME legal system: "If the contract is valid and binding, it shall not be permissible for either of the contracting parties to resile from it, nor to vary or rescind it, save by mutual consent or an order of the court, or under a provision of the law" (276 UAE law).

As a general rule in bilateral contracts, among which are numerous computer and IT contracts, the contract usually ends in many ways. One is the *natural end,* where everything goes well, and the contract is concluded normally (i.e. properly executed as agreed upon by both parties and their respective commitments have been fulfilled). In the case of definite contracts, this occurs with the expiration of the specified period. Should the contract duration not be defined (and in case of indefinite contracts), both parties shall be entitled to terminate the same with specific conditions (mainly allowing reasonable notice period and do not abusively terminate the contract).

On the other hand, should things go wrong, one of the parties resorts to terminate (revoke or rescind) the contract due to the failure of the other party to honour any of its contractual obligations. Revocation or rescission in this case is a remedy for breach of contract.

---

70 David Salt, Laura Warren, and Alex Hall from Clyde & Co Middle East "A guide to liquidated and ascertained damages for the Qatar construction scoter". Justine Reeves and Patrick Murphy from Clyde & Co, Dubai office. "English Contract Law" article articles on the internet.

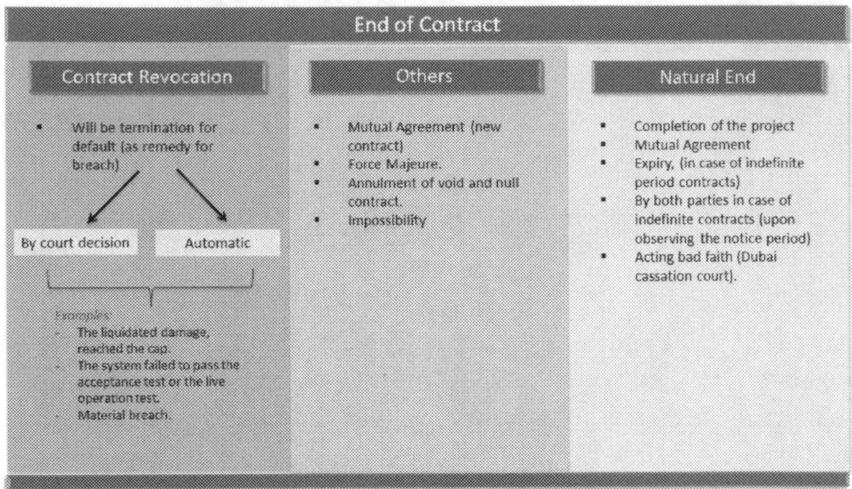

Figure 3: End of Contract

Revocation of contract is one of the means by which contract dissolution occurs, resulting in the removal or ending of the contractual bond linking the parties hereto. Here we would like to review this type of contract dissolution, as it frequently occurs in formulating and discussing the "termination" clause insofar as software contracts.

Revocation is a penalty or remedy for breach of a contractual obligation as well as a means by which the contractual bond may be dissolved upon the request of one party due to the other party's violation of contractual commitments. As such, revocation as a way to terminate the contract takes on two forms:

1) legal (or consensual) termination, which occurs by the authority of the law or automatically.
2) judicial revocation, which emanates by judicial order.

Consensual (or Automatic) Termination is documented by article 271 of the Emirati law (corresponding to article 158 of the Egyptian law, 210 of Kuwaiti law, and 184 of Qatari law), which allows to agree in the contract that the contract shall be regarded as being cancelled automatically without the need for a judicial order failing performance of the obligations arising there out, and such agreement shall not dispense with notice unless the contracting parties have expressly agreed that it should be dispensed with. Due to the serious out-turns of this type of termination; the following conditions must be fulfilled:

a) both parties must explicitly agree on the same while knowing well its serious implications and repercussions.
b) the breach or violation must be officially verified by notice to be sent to the defaulting party unless explicitly agreed otherwise.

This type of termination is rare to happen in practice; parties rather prefer to grant this right to one of the parties (or both) to be used at their discretion upon the occurrence of certain event(s) (for example, in case the system did not pass the repeated acceptance test).

Judicial Revocation (which occurs by virtue of a judicial order) has been described by article 272 of the UAE law (257/1 of the Egyptian law, article 209 of the Kuwaiti law), and states that: "(1) In contracts binding on both parties, if one of the parties does not do what he is obliged to do under the contract, the other party may, after giving notice to the obligor, require that the contract be performed or cancelled. (2) The judge may order the obligor to perform the contract forthwith or may defer (performance) to a specified time, and he may also order that the contract be cancelled (rescinded) and compensation to be paid in any case if appropriate".

Here we note the following:

- Termination (i.e. revocation) in this case only occurs in mutually binding contracts.
- The termination in this case is permissible only for the party suffering from the default (aggrieved party) as opposed to the defaulting party.
- The judge may not unilaterally issue a termination order on his own initiative; the party suffering from default must instigate it.
- Revocation constitutes an optional choice to the aggrieved party, since the text permits to request from the judge either

contract revocation, or specific performance of the defaulting party obligations. The judge is also authorized to defer the performance and allow the defaulting party more time.

- The party requesting revocation must not have breached any of its obligations.
- It is imperative to officially verify the breach (which could be either in full or part thereof) by sending an official notice to the defaulting party, while the judge enjoys discretional authority in the case of partial non-performance.
- Finally, the aggrieved party must be capable of accommodating the results of the revocation (i.e. to restore the situation to what it was prior at the time of contracting).

Key Point: The parties will be returned to the position they were in prior to entering into the contract. If this is not possible, the party suffering from the breach shall be entitled to request a judge to adjudicate a compensation that is commensurate to the damage it incurred.

Other ways of contract termination: Contract can also end in other ways, as follows:

Voidable Contract: where the contract has several defects in its formation, such as when the contract is violating the public order and morals. In this case, the end of the contract takes the form of annulment. The contract will be deemed as having never existed. In this case, the parties will restore the situation to what it was prior to the time of contracting.

Impossibility: the contract also can end if the fulfilment of the obligations becomes impossible due to some external cause (187-188 Qatari law, 173 UAE law).

The contract also can be terminated by consent of the parties, which in this case amounts to a cancellation, and with regard to a third party amounts to a new contract (269 UAE law).

The contract can be also terminated in case one of the parties fails to act in good faith as recently held by Dubai Court of Cassation (37/2008).

A final word on the contractual liability: the violation of contractual obligations carries immense and significant risks on both parties as follows:

On the defaulting party side: the implementation of the penalty clause, contract termination, confiscation of bank guarantee and performance securities, compensation (if not stipulated in the contract), or requesting its increase should the compensation value be deemed incommensurate with the incurred damage, the party stepping into the project, together with the moral damage occurred by a party's commercial repute, is responsible. The risks for the other party, who might not be innocent as well, include wasting company time, efforts, and money invested, let alone loss of the business benefits that were expected from the project.

From a practical approach to the matter, the failure of the contract will not only hurt the defaulting party but surpasses that to include irreparable damages to both parties, particularly if it leads to project collapse. The pertinent advice here indeed, in order to avoid such situation, is to encourage both parties to watch carefully at the outset what they promise before entering into the contract, and then fulfil precisely what they have been committed to, and carry on their obligations honourably in good faith.

Crying afterwards over spilled milk will not remedy the situation, and parties should know that applying the remedies stated by law would not retrieve what was being planned and dreamed to achieve, nor will it restore time, effort, money, and reputation wasted. This is in addition to the fact that contract termination may require restoring the situation of both parties to what it was prior to the agreement, which could prove challenging from a practical sense. Moreover, the limitation of liability provisions often stated in contracts makes project failure (contract termination by legal expression) imminent, and thus an actual calamity.

Conclusion: If I have to conclude the deep research performed in this chapter in few words, I would easily say that; contract is a formidable legal structure in its own right. Parties must admit the extremely significant legal structure and the power of contract. It is a versatile tool available to those involved in commercial activity. We encourage personnel in the software and IT industry to make themselves acquainted with the minimum requirements of contract basics that are closely related to practical reality. This will undoubtedly contribute to their efforts to avoid, mitigate or at a minimum deal with the risks and exposure embedded in software and IT projects.

=====================

Chapter 4
SOFTWARE AND IT CONTRACTS

Aim of the Chapter

This chapter strives to take a closer and more detailed look at the sources of risks present in IT projects by meticulously inspecting the structure and formation of software and IT contracts, while scrutinizing and dissecting the same. This is owing to the contract being a source of risk, as well as a tool for keeping those risks at bay. Throughout previous chapters we examined this subject and pointed out how a contract, or "contractual process", in theory, can play a vital role in mitigating the failure rate of software projects. Here we will proceed with an in-depth and scrupulous analysis, examining and dissecting the construction and formation of those contracts and the risks associated with them, and explain, in practical terms, how to use them to administer the overall risk in software and IT projects.

Preliminary Notes

1) Basic principles of the law of contracts are definitely applicable to software and IT contracts from an overall theoretical perspective. This simply means that whomever shall be vested with the responsibility of formulating or handling such contracts must be well versed in the relevant terms and principles. However, computer and IT contracts are unique in that they contain a set of special features, terms, and conditions that distinguishes them from other contracts. This is quite typical, owing to the nature of computer-related activities, together with the nature of this business and its markets. The truth is that software contracts have branched out, becoming varied and complex in their own right, and that warrants additional analysis and elaboration. However, this is not to say software and IT contracts fall outside the original rules and principals of the law of contracts. In fact, when dispute with one of those contracts arises, judges will not find any other principals to apply. This stipulates the need of comprehensive knowledge to the law of contracts and its applicability on the software and IT contracts as a new group of unnamed contracts.
2) The legal structure and commercial background of software and IT contracts are sometimes complex, owing to their association with advanced technologies and interrelated commercial ties, where numerous parties all play a role. This gives rise to varied legal relationships, where numerous products and services are availed and important issues are raised, such as intellectual property rights, data protection, integration, confidentiality and so forth. This becomes evident in contracts pertaining to the delivery of turnkey systems, which we shall refer to later, being closely linked to a unique feature of this industry, namely its universality. Clearly, the software industry has transcended regional borders for many reasons. One is that the major global players in the IT field are only a handful, and this has contributed to the widespread global mergers and acquisitions, as well as enforcing the rules of free international trade.

3) The manufacturers, providers, and suppliers of software and their consultants are quite experienced when it comes to computer and IT contracts, since most of these contracts are originally drafted by these individuals. This is quite a common phenomenon, as it is a domain with which they are the most knowledgeable and familiar. Consequently, this has led to commercial standards, customs, and initial drafting of these contracts to be set by the legal experts of such companies. As for clients, they are not indulged in this field, and perhaps a typical customer would only conclude a single computer deal once a year or so. In spite of this, however, some government organizations (especially in the West), together with other governmental agencies specialized in public purchases and procurement, actually develop contract forms, among which are computer and IT contracts. However, more often than not, these templates are rejected by providers, either due to their impartiality or because of some excessively strict clauses, or simply because they may not correspond well with the uniqueness of the information industry. This, however, should not be construed to undermine the significant and effective contribution made by clients (especially large companies in which IT systems are the backbone). In fact, this is especially true with regard to contracts pertaining to software development, website development, and other services.
4) There has been an increase in the number of categories under which computer and software contracts are divided, along with the diversification of the technologies associated with them, and due to their appeal to companies, organizations, and individuals. Moreover, the increase in commercial relations and the abundance of opportunities have led to an increase in demand for utilizing contracts in what has become known as the "battle of the forms".[71] In light of this, we recommend that only knowledgeable and experienced individuals be vested with the responsibility of drafting and negotiating such contracts. Preferably, these individuals should be well versed in the commercial and technical aspects of the industry, together

---

71 This phrase means that contracting parties are involved in a struggle for selecting the most appropriate contract form for the project, each from its own perspective and according to its negotiation position.

with the principles of international trade, the intentions of both parties, and what they seek to achieve.

We will now proceed to view how IT contracts can be used as a tool to help in controlling the risks associated with IT projects. This will necessitate examining in depth the structure of these contracts, their formation, and the risks associated with them, as well as other key elements of the mitigation plan drawn to keep such risks at bay.

General Considerations Surrounding IT Projects/Contracts[72]

The structure and formation of any contract are subject to a number of general considerations, which are themselves surrounding the project and are basis of the contract and accordingly a source of risk. Yet we notice that such considerations may vary according to how they are viewed and perceived in a given circumstances, and whether it is from the point of view of the client or from the perspective of the provider. The considerations we shall overview here constitute a common denominator between both parties of the contract, which they are obligated to view, not only when examining and analysing the risks but also during the contract discussion and negotiation phase. These considerations will determine the kind of negotiations and discussions that will take place regarding the contract, indeed will demonstrate the sensibility of the parties and their desire to remain aware of the project risks while working to cooperate for resolving them. This is especially true during the "contracting phase" as a cornerstone to the project lifetime.

The considerations at hand revolve around a number of questions that we believe are the main areas of risks that necessitate a greater attention, as follows:

Contract Subject Matter: What is it that we want from the contract/ project, and what are the products and services that constitute the subject and the essence of the contract? As a customer, what benefit

---

[72] The terms "project" and "contract" are used sometimes interchangeably, as the text may requires.

will I get out of signing the contract? As a provider, what are my undertakings and what am I obliged to deliver to the client?

When? What is the delivery date and implementation of the project? When will I, as a customer, be handed the system, product, or service that works as efficiently and effectively as I expect it to do? As a provider, when am I obligated to deliver the system, product, or service?

How Much? As a client, how much will I have to pay, and when and how? As a supplier, what is the payment I am expecting to receive, and when and how?

What Are the Anticipated Risks? Commercial, technical, legal, practical, and others, relevant to both parties.

Taking This Issue Further

The above can be detailed as follows:

Purpose of Contract: This part of the contract is a fundamental corner of the project/contract documents, around which other provisions revolve, and seeks to address the question of what is the substance of the contract, and why the parties signed the agreement initially. Does the purpose involve merely provisioning a set of technical and professional services, embodied in designing software? Or does it surpass this to include the design, implementation, and delivery of a complete and integrated IT system? Does it simply encompass a license for using specific software under specific terms and conditions, or management of the entire IT system on behalf of the client?

In order to avoid risks, we recommend, as an initial step, the compilation of a "project summary" by the technical personnel involved. This summary is supposed to be drafted in a simple and comprehensible language to outline an overall description of the project, without delving into the intrinsic technical details involved, together with the primary products and services offered by the project. We note here that this synopsis would be beneficial to the project team and would contribute to specifying the role of each party on the team. Further, this will help identify the right "contract form" (i.e. type or format of the appropriate project contract).

What Are the Other Vital Areas? Other relevant provisions: Upon specifying and outlining the contract scope, product, and services, the parties should address all other radical provisions and articles closely associated with the contract purpose, and which complete the contract as a significant tool for avoiding risks. These include delivery terms and conditions, system acceptance plan, time frame or schedule, supplier obligations, client obligations, guarantees and warranties extended by one party to another – specifically those concerning products and deliverables, warranties pertaining to system integration, service level agreements (in outsourced system management contracts and maintenance agreements), licensing terms and conditions, and project completion terms.

Key Point: As advised in every corner of this book, the detailed and accurate description of all relevant products and services ensures the elucidation of any possible ambiguities and prevention of numerous risks, thus averting disputes and assisting the parties in successfully executing the project at hand. The focus of the parties at this moment should be to produce coherent and robust contract.

The Contract's Greatest Beneficiary: Who is in the more powerful position? Is it the client who put all his trust in the provider? Or is it the provider, hoping his software will meet with the acceptance and recognition as a result of the project's success? Is it both? In other words, who is the powerful party when it comes to the negotiation table?

Who will insist upon the application of his own standard terms and conditions? Is it the provider, owing to its status as a renowned global company holding its ground, when all the customer can do is to approve? Or is it the other way round? Is the client a government agency or a private entity? **The best piece of advice** here would be that "winning and profiting is for all, just as failure and loss", which means that both parties have to focus on producing a fair and balanced contract that is impartial to either of them. They should also not overly burden the other party, bearing in mind that the project's success is a triumph for both of them, just as failure will affect them together.

Contract Value: Is it a large contract valued at millions with an execution period extending for years? Or is it a small contract having a short implementation plan? Large-size contracts are known to be afflicted by high failure rates. This is why we recommend dealing with high-value projects cautiously and professionally, while taking the necessary measures referred to in this book, as appropriate. This also includes other financial aspects such as customer credit, performance securities, tax burden, currency fluctuation, payment terms, conditions, and payment collection.

Technology and Technical Aspects: Does the contract involve complex and interrelated technologies – perhaps new technologies that have not yet been tried? Or is it related to simple technical matters entailing smaller risks? The more advanced and complicated technology you have used, the more potential risk you would experience.

Project Components and Integration: Where some projects involve the provision of several products (such as turnkey projects), these must work together in harmony just as expected of a coherent information system, within themselves or with other existing systems. The more project components, the more the need for integration and interoperability, because more risks will accordingly prevail.

Project Duration and Timeline: Is the project composed of several phases, each having a unique nature, circumstances, terms, and conditions? Or is it a one-off job? The greater the length of project duration, the greater the risk probability.

Suppliers and Providers: Will technologies and technical components be supplied by one provider or multiple ones? Multiple providers are common when it comes to IT projects, where hardware is provided by one supplier and software from another. Perhaps even the project management belongs to yet a third party. All contribute to the intricacies of these types of contracts and accordingly increase the risk level.

Cross-Border Implementation: Does project implementation transcend regional borders? More often than not contracts are concluded in one country yet are executed in another. Cross-border implementation raises the question of legal jurisdiction and means of dispute resolution, as well as some other types of risks such as logistics and taxation.

Documentation: Pertaining to the project, including the contract itself, these are always important for answering numerous issues and questions previously discussed, such as a checklist of system components, technical specifications, testing, and an acceptance plan. The means of documenting everything that has been agreed upon between the parties prior to the project initiation is a critical and decisive factor in diverting any possible risks associated with the IT project. In this regard, **we have to note** that contract documents are the only frame of reference between the parties. All discussions, correspondences, negotiations, and proposals before, during, or after the contracting phase have no value unless documented properly and added to the contract.

Others: There also exists another set of influential considerations that undoubtedly will help identify the risk and determine the structure of the contract and the discussions that transpire over it. They include the client's urgent needs and the existence of a tight deadline, hence the customer's acceptance of any term or condition for fulfilling such urgent demands. Conversely, the provider may also be desperate for winning new projects and thus his compliance with any terms and conditions regardless of how demanding they may be. Another factor pertains to the client's culture and the way executives and users perceive the provider, as a partner or otherwise. In addition, is the company a hopelessly bureaucratic one where decisions take an eternity to be made? On the other hand, is it an agile and efficient one characterized by a swift decision-making process? This is in addition to the role played by the history shared between both customer and provider, which will be vital in determining contract provisions and discussions. Other considerations include set budgets, internal corporate policies, knowledge degree of decision makers, as well as other factors that shall be discussed later; all are seeds of risks in IT contract, and accordingly IT projects.

As such, the source of risk confronting IT projects may be viewed from another prospect, that being the considerations surrounding the project at hand, which are outlined as follows:

Table 5: Source of Risk Confronting IT Projects from Different Prospects

Consideration	Risk	Prevention
Purpose of Contract (Scope of the Project)	This is the substance of the project. Misunderstanding the exact scope of the project is a major risk; it will affect most of the other contract areas, such as solution design, specifications, prices and payment, duration of the project, acceptance, and many others. This also will determine the type and form of the contract. One of the most prominent risks is erring in the selection of the appropriate contract form.	Outlining an accurate detail of the scope of contract, products, and services, including the description of system deliverables, specifications, and specifying exclusions. Understanding the overall aspects of the project and selecting the right contract form accordingly.
Other Vital Areas	Another significant risk is caused by the misinterpretation of any other vital areas that are closely related and/or associated with the purpose of the contract. Due to the stark variation of IT projects, respective vital areas also differ to a great extent.	Next in importance comes the accurate depiction of other vital areas that are closely related to contract scope, products and services. These include protection of intellectual property rights of the parties, warranties and representations, service level, license terms and conditions, delivery dates, acceptance tests, project completion conditions, confidentiality, penalties, responsibilities, termination, and conflict resolution.

Negotiation Status	It is possible that one of the parties could command a more superior negotiation status than its counterpart (such as being the sole supplier of a product that the client badly requires), and so impose its own terms in a manner that disrupts the delicate balance of the contract.	Excessive and unrealistic commitment is the seed for assured failure. An impartial and just balance must be established between the parties, insofar as obligations, commitments, and risks are concerned. Having a balanced and fair business relation is one of the secrets of project success. Another secret is the sincere cooperation between parties with one objective: to succeed.
Contract Value, Duration, and Size	Studies and statistics have pointed out that large-scale projects (in terms of value and duration) are more prone to failure in comparison to smaller projects.	Study vigilantly the finance-related issues and take the necessary measures to mitigate the risks. Reduce the project size or divide it into phases while considering each phase an independent project in its own right.
Technology and Technical Aspects	A new technology that has not been previously manifested constitutes another project risk.	Specialized technicians must perform a technical study and proof of concept to ensure the applicability of the proposed technology on a practical level. Manifestation of the concept is a must.
Integration and Data Issues	Another substantial risk lies in the project being composed of numerous elements, whose integration and harmonious operation remains in doubt, whether among themselves or among the existing systems. Data to be transferred from the legacy system is a major risk.	Ensuring the integration and seamless operation of project components by the virtue of a sound technical study and analysis. More focus to the data issue in the brownfield systems is required.

Suppliers and Sub Contractors	The presence of multiple suppliers, coupled with the lack of predetermined relation and coordination between them, poses another potential risk for the project.	Place relationships with suppliers and subcontractors under the management of a single party. Adjust and confirm such relations with third parties beforehand.
Cross-Border Projects	The cross-border projects pose problems pertaining to logistics, legal jurisdiction, and unfamiliarity with local legislation, regional circumstances, and conflict resolution. For this reason, they constitute an obvious risk area.	These types of projects require tremendous efforts for regulating the commercial and legal relationship between the parties and study the surrounding circumstances separately.
Documentation	Neglecting to document what has been agreed upon during the negotiation phase in a professional and methodical manner paves the way for conflicts and disputes, thus creating a clear and imminent risk. This similarly applies to documentation during the project.	The points agreed upon between the parties must be recorded accurately, in a well-drafted legal document before and during project implementation phases.
Others	Limited time designated to the negotiation phase and agreement documentation. Determine whether or not the client's organization is a cooperative one and how swiftly the decisions are made therein. Insufficient resources or an unqualified project team is a major risk.	The project team must be granted ample time to complete negotiations and document agreements. Cooperation between contract parties does not merely constitute customary practice; it is also one of the factors ensuring project success. Ensure there are enough skilled and qualified project team members. A backup plan must be in place to overcome resource turnover.

From the above, we can easily notice that the risk is there and may be greater whenever:

- The scope is not clear, well-defined, or rightly expressed.
- The size of the project is big, the duration is lengthy, and the value is high.
- The technology used in the project is new or complicated.
- The vendors and suppliers are many and not well connected.
- The project components, phases, products, and services are high in number.
- The implementation of the project is outside the territory.
- The contract documentation is not comprehensive and accurate enough.
- The overall balance between the parties is fractured.
- The project involves complicated integration, interfaces, and old data migration.

Key Point: A general word of advice here is that; the above considerations and risks associated should be studied and evaluated, – preferably by a specialized and impartial external party vested with the responsibility of identifying, analysing, and assessing the considerations and influential factors previously mentioned. This is together with determining the risk degree of each and adding any other special risk (such as economic circumstances or political turmoil in a particular country).

All relevant parties are required to fully cooperate with this specialized entity and furnish it with all the imperative data and information required for achieving accurate results. The objective of such exercise is to draw a comprehensive plan, for risk identification, treatment and mitigation, before the start of the project yet before signing the contract. The plan must also identify the responsible personnel for the implantation and control of the plan.

Software and IT Contracts: Formation Analysis

Now we shall delve more deeply into the realm of software and IT contracts and closely examine the provisions of these contracts by analysing, dissecting, and familiarizing ourselves with them so we are better able to utilize them. In doing so, we shall see how we might utilize the texts for dealing with risks, mitigating their impact, and attempting to increase the project's chances for success. It is our conviction that the effective and proper formulation of provisions is one of the best-kept secrets for ensuring successfully executed software and IT projects.

Two Types of IT Contracts

This book examines two distinct types of IT contracts. The first are pure IT contracts that are directly associated with an IT project, product, or a related service. They are *core* to the software and IT industry. This category includes licensing agreements, software development, maintenance and technical support, integrated IT systems, IT outsourcing, and the like. The other type of contract is not considered a software and IT contract per se, but it is indeed *contiguous* to the industry and is frequently used, such as in confidentiality agreements, IT employment contracts, escrow agreements, and so forth. The cynosure of this book is the IT contracts.

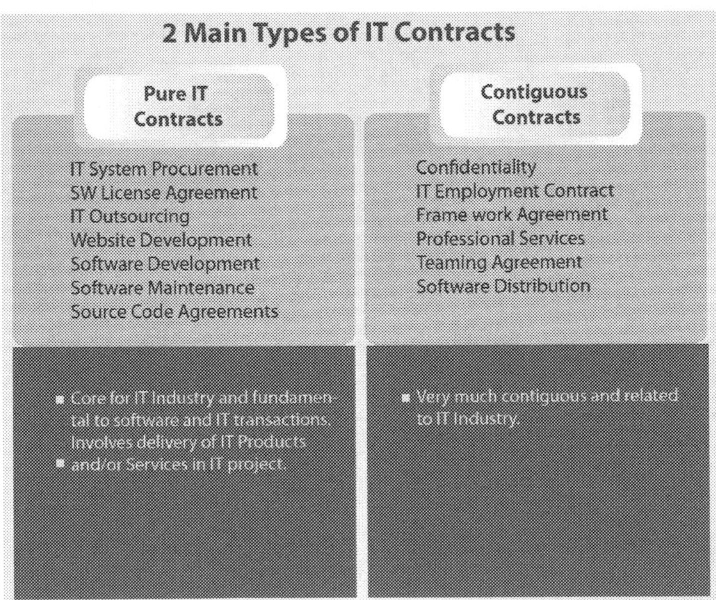

Figure 4: 2 Main Types of IT Contracts.

Three Types of Provisions: Inevitably, certain terms are more significant to the contracts than others. If we were to consider software and IT contracts in a general sense, we would find these revolving around three types (or levels) of provisions:

- **Core Provisions**: These are fundamental to the transaction and purpose of the contract. In fact, they are the core of the core (i.e. the core provision of the core IT contracts). Clauses clarify and explain the scope of contract and other fundamental and core areas of the project. These provisions are often rather technical in nature and are mainly associated with the scope, specifications, time, and method of implementation and the like. Another attribute is that since they are fundamental and the breach of which may destroy the purpose of the contract, such a breach will be considered a material breach. For all of the above, such clauses constitute the primary source of risk. Examples include product or service description, contract deliverables, party responsibilities, system testing and acceptance, specifications, system design, system description for turnkey projects, and texts pertaining to maintenance operations.
- **General Provisions**: These are the principal texts in any contract structure, and are often characterized by a more legal or commercial nature. They are imperative for drafting a complete and comprehensive contract, together with enabling the parties to familiarize themselves with all aspects of the project at hand. However, they are ancillary in terms of relation to project completion since they are not related to the core of the project. (See the following figure, which depicts a spectrum of clauses to be outlined later.)
- **Standard Provisions:** These too are basic provisions but appear throughout the contract in a generic way. Yet in spite of software and IT contracts having such provisions in common with other contracts in other industries, they are still worthy of consideration.

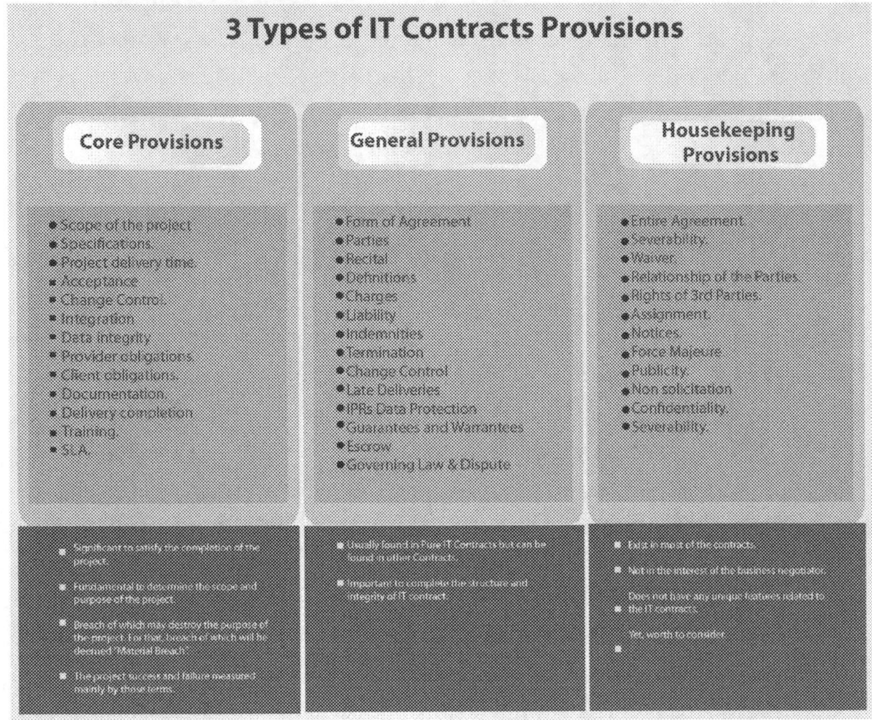

Figure 5: 3 Types of IT Contracts Provisions

The following table shows the distribution of the three types of provisions in some of the "pure IT contracts".

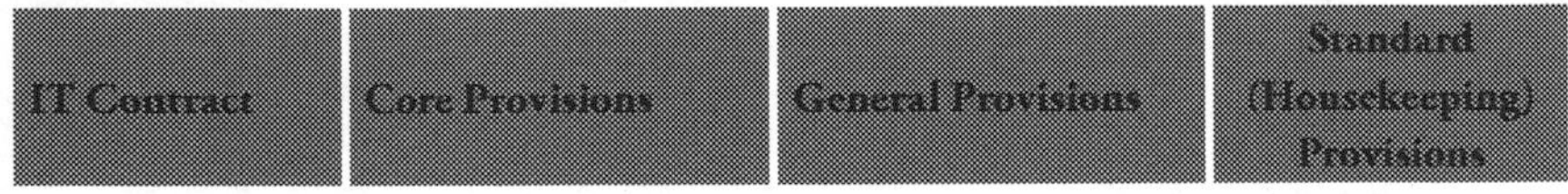

IT Contract	Core Provisions	General Provisions	Standard (Housekeeping) Provisions

IT Turnkey System	- **Scope of the project** - System description - Items to be provided - Project timetable - Project duration - Parties' obligations - Delivery & installation - Acceptance testing - Specifications - System integration - Data protection - Data migration **Schedules:** • *Scope of services and deliverables* • *Acceptance testing* • *Technical support services* • *Project plan* • *Gap analysis* • *Specifications* • *Acceptance certificates* • *Hardware*	- **Form of agreement** - Parties - Definition - List of contractual documents - Project management - System price - Charges & payments - Support & maintenance - License rights - Training - Title & risk - Warranties - Ownership of the software - Indemnities - Change control - Termination - Limitation of liability - Insurance - Software license - Escrow arrangements - No soliciting	- **Force majeure** - Assignment - Notices - Entire agreement - Severability - Waiver - Relation of the parties Rights of 3rd parties publicity Governing law - Dispute resolution - Confidentiality

IT Outsourcing	- Scope of services - Service level - Parties obligations - Employees & asset transfer - 3rd parties projects & contracts - Transition period & plan - Transformation - Warranties - Technology update - Exit Plan **Schedules:** *Price book* *Scope of services* *Schedule & staffing* *Responsibility matrix* *Due diligence report and assumptions* *Deliverables* *Governance and escalation structure* *Penalty/reward* *Structure and exclusion List* *Change management reporting* *Service level* *Business transfer* *Agreement* *(assets/employees transfer)*	- Form of agreement - Parties - Definition - List of contract documents - Duration - Charges & payments - License rights - Governance & project control - Training - Penalties & bonuses - Indemnities - Change control - Termination - Limitation of liability - Right to audit - IPRs indemnity - Data protection and privacy - No soliciting	- Force majeure - Assignment - Notices - Entire agreement - Severability - Waiver - Relation of the parties - Rights of 3rd party publicity - Governing law - Dispute resolution confidentiality

Software License	- Definition of software - Who is licensing the software? - Who is authorized to use the software? - Duration - Scope of license - Authorized uses - Delivery, installation & acceptance **Schedules:** • *Equipment* • *Software* • *Fees*	- Form of license (agreement) - Parties - Definitions - Maintenance (period, fees, scope) - Indemnification - Limitation of liabilities - Protection and security - Training - License fees - Warranties - Escrow arrangement	- Force majeure - Assignment - Notices - Entire agreement - Severability - Waiver - Relation of the parties - Rights of 3rd parties' publicity - Governing law - Dispute resolution - Confidentiality
Software Maintenance	- Scope of maintenance services - Managing maintenance operation - Excluded services - Service level agreement - Services charges - Charges for excluded services - Parties obligations	- Form of agreement - Definitions - Duration - Proprietary rights and license - Confidentiality - Term - Liability - Assignment - Subcontract - Employees solicitation	- Force majeure - Assignment - Notices - Entire agreement - Severability - Waiver - Relation of the parties - Rights of 3rd parties - publicity - Governing law - Dispute resolution - Confidentiality

Software Development	- Software to be developed - Obligations of the parties - Delivery and installation - Project plan - Project management - Testing and acceptances **Schedules:** • *Equipment* • *The software* • *The services* • *Payment/price* • *locations* • *Implementation/ project plan* • *Outline specification* • *Project personnel* • *Manuals* • *Training* • *Escrow Agreement* • *Statement of work* • *Software license terms* • *Maintenance and support* • *Service levels* • *Change control*	- Form of agreement - Parties - Definitions - Key Staff - Information and access - Price and payment - License the software to the customer - Training - Escrow arrangement - Change control	- Force majeure - Assignment - Notices - Entire agreement - Severability - Waiver - Relation of the parties - Rights of3rd parties publicity - Governing law - Dispute resolution - Confidentiality

Software Distribution	- Appointment of distributor - Term - Supplier responsibilities - Distributor responsibilities - Supply of the products **Schedules** • *Software, equipment, minimum numbers of copies license fees and charges* • *Technical information* • *Software license agreement* • *Supplier support* • *Terms and charges to distributor*	- Form of agreement - Parties - Definitions - Software licensing - IPRs - Warranties - Termination - Confidentiality - Liability - General	- Force majeure - Assignment - Notices - Entire agreement - Severability - Waiver - Relation of the parties - Rights of 3rd party publicity - Governing law - Dispute resolution - Confidentiality
Software Escrow	- Definitions of materials to be deposited - Timing of deposit Materials - Release of deposit materials - Termination	- Form of agreement - Parties - Recital - Definitions - Term - Fees - Indemnities - Developer warranties and representations	- Force majeure - Assignment - Notices - Entire agreement - Severability - Waiver - Relation of the parties - Rights of 3rd party publicity - Governing law - Dispute resolution - Confidentiality

Table 6: Distribution of the Three Types of Provisions in some of the Software and IT Contracts.

Here we should always note that the selection of such provisions (as shown in the table above) is not a complete list, but it represents the ones prevalent in most of the IT contracts in one way or another. It may differ with respect to project and case, based on the surrounding circumstances. The differentiation among the three types is the author's personal assessment based on his or her personal experience.

Despite the benefits of the above classification, nothing to say that a group is less important than the other is. Each one of the three types of the above provisions is by itself and by its very nature a source of risk. Arguably, any error, defect, negligence, or poor drafting will be a seed of the failure tree; only the degree of risk may differ from one group to another and from one project to another based on circumstances and factors.

Standard Provisions

These are common provisions found in all computer and IT contracts, in addition to being present in other industries' contracts. Examples include:

Entire Agreement is the provision excluding any previous negotiations, discussions, correspondences, or agreements between the parties, or any other documents preceding the contract. It goes on to affirm the entirety of the contract, meaning that no other preceding agreements or documents shall hold weight. It also stipulates that any amendment or modification can only take effect upon the written consent of both parties. The objective of this provision is to deter either party from referring to any previous document or agreement outside the framework of the contractual agreement. Therefore, and with the presence of this clause, the parties should include – in the contract – all agreements and documents deemed necessary for the project at hand.

Severability refers to the concept that if one of the articles proves null and void, this shall not affect the validity of the contract in its entirety. Article 211/1 of the UAE law provides, "If part of the contract is void, the entire contract shall be void unless the subject matter of each part is separately specified, in which case it shall be void as to the void part, and the remainder shall be valid" (corresponding to the article 143 Egyptian law and article 190 Kuwaiti law).

Waiver: The article that stipulates that should one of the parties not utilize any of the rights mentioned herein, then this shall not be construed as a waiver of those rights. If the parties agree that the supplier should deliver specific goods at a set date, and if the supplier so fails and the buyer upholds the contract and requests a new delivery date, then this shall not mean that the buyer has waived his right to claim compensation delay, if applicable. This is true for any other right authorized by the contract.

Rights of third Parties regulates the rights of other parties if any, and most probably excludes third parties from benefiting from the contract.

Assignment: This clause regulates whether it is possible for one party to assign its rights to a third party, with the contract remaining in effect. The rule here is that any party may assign its rights to another one, unless otherwise stipulated by the contract, and unless the contract type (such as license contracts) prevents them from doing so.

Another clause is the one pertaining to **notices**, which aims to identify the address to which notices should be legally directed, which is an important piece of information overlooked by many, especially in the event of a conflict or dispute.

Force Majeure: This clause deals with force majeure and how it affects the performance and obligations of the parties.

We notice here that standard provisions are always backed by the significant legal theories, which are sometimes technically quite complex. It is not within the scope of this book to go into the depth of those theories. In spite of the importance of these provisions, many contracting parties still continue to overlook them and do not give them the recognition they deserve. Each one of the provisions addresses a special circumstance, its importance, becoming apparent with the emergence of each addressed case.

Software and IT Contracts Groups

Due to the growth and development of the computer industry and an increasing volume of local and global interaction through hardware and software, an extensive array of contracts has emerged, all dealing with various aspects of computer-related transactions. These contracts possess a number of unique features and set of clauses and provisions that set them apart and deem them worthy of study and examination.

Apparently, computer contracts cannot be accurately quantified due to the varying commercial activities and transactions in the computer field and their perpetual increase. However, we may be able to categorize these contracts into groups based on the main activities and transactions in IT industry as previously described in Chapter 1 (i.e. hardware, software, systems, services, Internet, and database), whereby each group represents a group of transactions.

My obvious ***piece of advice*** here is to apprehend the different categories of software and IT contracts and the types within each category: when and how to use them (i.e. which form to be used in which transaction) because failure to use the right form is one of the potential risks in contracting for IT projects. Another piece of advice is that each group should be given a title or heading so that when picking up a contract, one can see the title and know what it is likely to contain and when and how it can be used.

This is an example of classifying the software and IT contracts in groups:

Hardware		Hardware sales Hardware maintenance Hardware lease Networking and infrastructure
Systems		System procurement (turnkey) System integration services management System maintenance and support

Software		Software procurement Software development - *Agreement for software development and licensing* - *Computer games development agreement* - *Joint software development agreement* Software maintenance Software marketing/distribution - *OEM*[1] *VAR*[2] - Software Escrow - *Multi licensee software escrow agreement* - *Single licensee software escrow agreement* - *Single licensee website and software escrow agreement* - *Information escrow agreement* Asset Purchase/Assignment - *Software purchase agreement* - *General IPRs assignment* - *Asset purchase agreement* Software License - *Software license code* - *End-user license agreement* - *Beta test/trail evaluation* - *Shrink-wrap license* - *Click-wrap license*
Services		Maintenance and support Managed service Service level agreement Professional services IT outsourcing Master service agreement Consultancy Software services
Internet and Database		Internet services provider Website development Website software license Website hosting Application software provider Database license Database purchase Trans boarder data flow Content provider

Frame Agreements		Master purchase agreement Frame agreement (IT procurement) Frame agreement (IT outsourcing)
Others		Memorandum of understanding Strategic alliance Teaming agreement Proprietary notice Non-Disclosure and confidentiality agreement Agreements related to IT employees

Table 7: Software and IT Contracts Grouping

Battle of Forms

It is not possible or feasible for the parties to draw up a contract from scratch. Instead, more often than not negotiations will start based on a previously formulated contract proposed by one of the parties. It could be the supplier who believes his forms match the industry standards and fulfils the goals and safeguards interests from his perspective. On the other side, it is possible that the user has a similar contract form, and to perceive that (sometimes) as a buyer, he could be in a better position to impose his contract form as a foundation to begin the negotiation process. This is when the "battle of the forms" emerges, where each party fights to impose its own form. Certainly, the party whose conditions are adopted as the basis for negotiation will have the upper hand, since the discussions will revolve around its pre-set terms and conditions.

Practically, the other party will not have much room to manoeuvre, because -for instance- the client's contract form may entail additional services, a more extensive scope, increased burdens on the supplier, more responsibilities, additional guarantees or excessive penalties. It is unlikely that any supplier will accept this, except in return for an increase in price to cover the risks he may be exposed to as a result. Generally, it is unlikely that a supplier would accept the terms that surpass his capabilities or resources, as this could result in a grossly imbalanced contract and thus a sure loss or an inevitable failure of the project. If the client approves this flaw, then the parties have no one to blame but themselves, having signed an "impartial and imbalanced contract" that will inevitably lead to a mutual loss and failure.

Standard Forms and Precedents

Standard forms are a legal documents, and contracts redrafted for future use, while precedents are legal documents and contracts used in previous incidents. In general, the presence of pre-drafted standard contracts, provisions, or precedents, regardless of the battling parties, is in itself a matter abundant with benefits and advantages:

- Compiling and developing a previously formulated contract gives the drafter many opportunities to familiarize himself with the overall framework and potentially vital aspects of the project at hand. This way, all that is up for discussion will be limited to details pertaining to technical, financial, commercial, and legal aspects of a particular transaction. The availability of the correct form and impartial framework helps both parties to avoid known traps and pitfalls greatly assists them in rendering a "coherent and fair" contract, leading to a "successful project".
- From the supplier's side, the existence of standard provisions is an extremely important matter, especially in relation to the protection of software property rights and trade secrets. This is because existing laws may not provide the required protection, whereas through these standard provisions, intellectual protection may be detailed to render appropriate protection to the software involved. Areas of particular vitality here include suitable licensing conditions, safeguarding the source code, escrow arrangement with a third party, and so forth. Such matters are not only the supplier's interests but are also advantageous for the user, insofar as becoming familiar with these new terms and capitalizing on their provisions.
- Standard contracts and provisions are also beneficial in that when deals with projects of small value or content, they do not require extensive discussions or negotiations, simple contract form is sufficient.

- When dealing with government institutions, you often find that these organizations have pre-set contract forms, which they utilize in the event of tenders or public procurement and purchasing. Standard provisions are often included and the chances of negotiating over these are frequently low.
- Finally, from a historical perspective, credit for laying the groundwork of computer and IT contract forms should be given to lawyers and legal consultants in the United States. This is where the industry originated, and even now with the dissemination of technology and increased expertise of customers, we still feel that the United States remains a reference point in the field.

Key Point: Professionals must be careful when using pre-drafted standard or precedents, as they can be a double-edged sword. It should be no more than valuable reminder of the provisions commonly used in particular transaction. It is dangerous to assume that a form or precedent can be used for all transaction. All precedents must be reviewed carefully, tested, improved, tailored, and customized for each specific transaction. A good standard form may embody decades of experience.[73]

73 Paul Rylance, *Legal Writing and Drafting*, Blackstone Press Limited.113.

Chapter 5
CONTRACTING FOR TURNKEY PROJECTS

Aim of the Chapter

The main objective of the previous chapters was "setting the scene", in which we delineated the idea of the new approach, its construction, and effects. Now proceeding one step further, we apply the new approach to one of the most important activities in the software and IT industry, the "turnkey project". Here we see how it works, how the contract (or the contractual processes) can, in actuality, be an effective tool to manage the risk and enhance the chances of success of the project. What type of steps, measures, and precautions should be taken during the contractual processes to achieve the intended target of the project? In addition, this chapter offers rich information about the business and legal environment of IT turnkey projects.

Background

A turnkey project,[74] in the realm of software and IT, means the design, supply, delivery, installation, operation, guarantee, and maintenance of an information system that performs specific functions in a specific work environment. The word *system* or *solution* means an integrated system of software, hardware, and services professionally combined to solve a functional problem or run operations automatically in any given business environment. The premise is that the system is designed and required to perform a main function of an institution.

IT projects range from those of simple size and value, as a simple computer program that fulfils a defined purpose or helps solve a specific problem, and may not require a great effort in installation, operation and maintenance, to more sophisticated and sensitive systems such as those used in banks, communications, defence, aviation, etc. The size and complexity of an information system reflects its financial value, time of execution, and the ways and methodologies of execution, maintenance, and managed services, which require technical and practical skills and experience as well as various business knowledge. As we noticed before, the high value and size projects usually involve greater risk.

Key Point: It should be noted here that software and IT projects referred to in this book are projects that, to a great extent, fall within the turnkey projects category. Accordingly, when we talk about the high rate of failure in IT projects, we mean the high rate of failure in turnkey projects. Risk and exposure in other types of projects such as IT outsourcing, license, software development, and others will be discussed in volume two of this book.

[74] Called turnkey, as a customer eventually receives a complete and integrated deliverable, thus the customer just needs to "turn the key". They are also called systems integration, for integration is the most important component and the most prominent feature in the turnkey systems. They are also called systems procurement or total solution, while companies operating in this field are called systems providers.

What Makes These Projects Risky?

Projects related to integrated information systems, or turnkey systems, is a puzzle by its very nature, and is one of the most important and complex subjects in the IT industry and computer contracts domain, simply because it usually presents the following risk features:

These projects include computer hardware, software (programs and databases), networks, and a huge range of services such as designing, installing, operating, and training, maintaining, providing technical support for, and linking the components together in an integrated system. Such components, including data issues, call for special technical expertise in each field in addition to other commercial and executive experiences that include legal expertise in drafting the related legal documents and contracts. The area of IT turnkey projects comes to light as a spectacular combination between technology and human resources, and wonderful interaction between business, technology, and legal expertise.

Most of the projects include a considerable amount of software development and customization, which constitutes the main element of these projects. Such processes are aimed at fulfilling the needs and requirements of a customer as per his business nature, knowing that software development is one of the most risky areas in the software industry, as this area in particular may constitute the cause of a higher probability of failure of IT projects.

Certainly in such projects, a company or a supplier cannot solely design and execute the information system. There must be concerted efforts of various parties with different areas of experience. Such parties may be from different countries, creating overlapping relationships and consequently, more complexity.

The execution periods for such projects can be prolonged, as they may take several years, during which an information system can be fully or partially replaced. Also, during the course of this period, the management, convictions, moods, views, and directions may change.

This can affect the progress of the project or even change the technology by which the project was built.

The above facts inevitably cause these projects to come in at a higher cost from every direction, and accordingly a high potential risk.

Main Features of Turnkey Projects

In fact, these projects are considered the backbone of the IT industry and are mainly the concern when we talk about software and IT projects. In addition to the above features, which by themselves are the areas of risk, these projects contain a number of factors that cause these to be associated with high risk, especially the larger sized, including:

(A) Level of technology and technical issues
(B) Number of components of the project (hardware, software, services)
(C) Number of suppliers and providers playing roles in the execution of the system
(D) A customer's effective participation and active involvement in the implementation and success of the project
(E) The integration between the components of the system, and between it and other existing systems
(F) Data issues in general, including migration from the old to the new system

Due to the above features, we notice a higher level of risk involved with the turnkey information system projects, whether at the time of contracting or at the time of execution, whether on the part of customers who put their trust in one contractor to get a state-of-the-art IT system, or on the part of the contractor, who is exposed to a huge legal responsibility.

Legal Nature of the Turnkey Agreement

According to the prevailing opinion in jurisprudence in ME, countries that adopt the civil code legal system, the turnkey contracts, are considered to fall under the "contract for work" (*Muqawala* in legal Arabic terminology) class of contracts. This type of contract is one that has been given a specific name by the law, and whose special provisions have been highlighted in some detail by the provisions of the civil code. This contract exists in all ME civil codes under the same name. Article 872 of the UAE civil law, 646 of the Egyptian code, and 661 of the Kuwaiti law state: "Muqawala is a contract whereby one of the parties thereto undertakes to make a thing or perform work in consideration which the other party undertakes to provide". Article 661 of the Kuwaiti civil code added "without being a delegate of or affiliated with the other party".

To be described as Muqawala, the main grounds on which the agreement must be designed is to create a legal binding relation in which one of the parties has to do work or perform services for the other party independently, against agreed compensations. Accordingly, this type of contract carries **two main criteria,** which differentiate it from other similar contracts where the main purpose is to perform work (such as employment contract): **a)** the work or the task to be done should be performed *independently*; **b)** this work or thing is performed against *consideration*. Once satisfied, the contract will be subjected to the pre-organized provisions of such named contracts in the civil codes.

These types of contracts feature two distinctive characteristics:

(i) One Debtor: In most cases, the Muqawala contract has only one contractor committed to deliver the integrated system. Said contractor is responsible for coordination and supervision of subcontractors, if any, and is consequently liable to the customer for the whole project.

(ii) Integration: A feature that prescribes the indivisibility of the obligations under the contract. It means that although the subject of the contract (the project) involves different components, elements, and various suppliers, the contract considers that the obligations arising from these components and elements are integrated and interconnected. So the contractor is responsible for the contractual components to be integrated, in business term: "on a turnkey basis".

Something to Think About: If the IT turnkey project is perceived as a Muqawala agreement, (most in the ME probably will) the parties' relationship – in the absence of the parties' specific agreements – will be governed and subjected to the provisions of the Muqawala agreements as stipulated in the civil codes. Among these provisions, as far as IT projects are concerned, are the provisions of contract definitions, effects of the Muqawala contract, obligations of both parties, warrantees under Muqawala, contractor liability, subcontracting, and the end of Muqawala. Without going into the details of the provisions of the Muqawala as stipulated in the civil codes, there is no doubt that the IT turnkey system projects were not in the mind of the legislators (or even other jurists and those who studied law) at the time of drafting these provisions, as these projects were not known or common at the time of legislation, and the legislator had nothing in his mind or perception of, other than the Muqawala agreements in their normal sense (construction, architectural, civil engineering and electrical, etc.).

This matter presents another area of risk which requires a separate independent and deliberate study of the extent to which the provisions of the Muqawala agreements apply to the information technology projects given the special nature of this industry and a huge gap between the current legal system and the actual daily practice as well as the rapid development of IT industry. Following some Muqawala principals as stipulated in the ME civil codes, which may or may not match the standards in IT industry, and accordingly may or may not apply in case of software and IT contracts. Here we admit that the parities enjoy a vast freedom to agree on anything so long as the subject matter is possible and in compliance with public order and general moral and decency and not violating an authoritative rule of the law:

- **Provide Work and/or Materials**: The contractor may provide only the work on the condition that the employer provides the materials. It is also permissible for the contractor to provide the materials and the work (873 UAE, 647/1, 2 Egypt, 662 Kuwait).

- **Description of the Contract Subject Matter**: The subject matter of the Muqawala contract must be described, particularly its kind, amounts thereof, the manner of performance, and the period over which it is to be performed. The consideration must be specified (874 UAE) and must be *defined or capable of being defined so as to rule out the complete ignorance*, otherwise the whole contract will be considered null and void.
- **Quality of the Work**: If parties agree that the contractor should provide the materials for the work, either in whole or in part, he shall be liable for the quality thereof in accordance with contract if any, or in accordance with current practice (875/1 UAE, 649/1 Egypt). As of the language of the Kuwaiti law, if the materials are provided by the contractor in all or in part, they must comply with the agreed specifications. If the specifications are not explicitly mentioned in the contract, they must be good and enough for the fulfilment of the intended purpose. The contractor warrants the defects in the materials which are difficult to discover upon the delivery of the work, as per the provisions of defects warranty of selling items (663 Kuwait).
- **Employer Provides the Materials:** If it is the employer who is bound to provide the materials for the work, the contractors must take due care of them and observe proper technical standards in his work, and return the balance of the materials to the owner, and if he makes default and the materials are destroyed, damaged, or lost, he shall be liable (875/2 UAE, 649/1 Egypt, (664 Kuwait).
- **Contract Appurtenant**: The contractor must provide at his own expense such additional equipment and tools which are necessary to complete the work, unless there is an agreement or custom to the contrary (876 UAE, 649/1 Egypt, 666 Kuwait).
- **Contractor's none (or Delay) of Performance**: The contractor must complete the work in accordance with the conditions of the contract. If it appears he is carrying out what he has undertaken in a defective manner, or in a manner that breaches the agreed conditions, the employer may require a contract be

terminated immediately if it is impossible to make good the work. But if it is possible to make good the work, it shall be permissible for the employer to require the contractor to abide by the conditions of the contract and to repair the work within a reasonable period.

If such a period expires without the reparation being performed, the employer may apply to the judge for the cancellation of the contract. The contractor shall be liable or is responsible to engage another contractor to complete the work at the expense of the first contractor (877 UAE, 650/1 Egypt, 667/1,2 Kuwait). Under Egyptian and Kuwaiti laws, the employer can ask for an immediate termination if the reparation is impossible. The Kuwaiti law allows the judge to refuse the rescission of the contract in case the defect in the way of execution will not reduce to a great extent the work value or its capability for the intended use, notwithstanding the right to claim compensation if appropriate (667/3).

- **Contractor Liability**: The contractor shall be liable for any loss or damage resulting from his action or work whether through his wrongful default or not, but he shall not be liable if it arises out of an event which could not have been prevented (878 UAE).
- **Work Delivery**: The employer shall be bound to take delivery of the work done when the contractor has completed it and places it at his disposal, and if, without any lawful reason, he (employer) refuses despite being given an official notice to take delivery, if the property is destroyed or damaged in the hands of the contractor without any wrongful act or default on his part, the contractor shall not be liable (884 UAE, 655 Egypt, 672 Kuwait).
- **Completion of the Work**: Once the work has been accomplished and put under the disposal of the employer, and the contractor so notified the employer, the employer shall be liable to take delivery of the work in accordance with the common practice. If the employer refuses to do so without any legitimate reason, the delivery will be deemed done 672 Kuwait).

- **Abstain from Delivery by Employer**: The employer may abstain from taking delivery of the work, if the gravity of the defect or violation in breach of the agreed terms makes the work incapable for use (673/1 Kuwait). If the defect does not reach such a grave level, the employer can only request reduction of the consideration in proportion of the importance of the defect, or order the contractor to repair the defect in a reasonable period to be determined by him, if the repair is possible without an extensive cost (673/2 Kuwait). In all cases, the contractor may do the repair in a reasonable time if doing so is possible and does not cause harm of high value (63/3 Kuwait).
- **Change of Orders:** If the Muqawala contract is made on the basis of an agreed plan in consideration of a lump-sum payment, the contractor may not demand any increase over the lump sum as may arise out of the execution of such plan (887/1 UAE, 658/1 Egypt). If any addition or amendment is made to the plan with the consent of the employer, the existing agreement with the contractor must be observed in connection with such variation or additions (887/2 UAE, 568/2 Egypt).
- **Increase of Materials Price:** If the prices of the raw materials, labour, and other costs increase, the contractor is not allowed to ask for an increase of the contract price, even if such an increase in the cost of materials is high to the extent that it makes the execution of the contract difficult (658/3 Egypt, 679 Kuwait).
- **General Exceptional Accidents**: If the economic balance between the obligations of the contractor and the employer collapses as a result of general exceptional accidents which were unforeseen at the time of signing the contract, and such accidents result in the collapse of the basis on which the Muqawala contract was established, the judge may increase the contract consideration or adjudicate the rescission of the contract (658/4 Egypt).
- **Subcontracting**: The contractor may subcontract the whole or part of the work to a subcontractor provided there is no condition in the contract preventing him from doing so, or the nature of the work mandates him to perform the work himself. In such a case, the first contractor shall remain liable as towards the employer (890 UAE, 661 Egypt, 681 Kuwait).

A subcontractor shall have no claim against the employer for anything due him from the first contractor unless he has made an assignment to him against the employer (891 UAE). Contrary to this, articles 662 Egypt and 682 Kuwait allow subcontractors and workers of the contractor to claim their due amounts towards the contractor from the employer directly, but such claims will be limited only to the due to the original contractor from the employer.

- **Termination of Muqawala:** A contract of Muqawala shall terminate upon the completion of the work agreed to or upon the cancellation of the contract by the consent or order of the court (892 UAE). If any cause arises preventing the performance of the contract or the completion of the performance thereof, either of the contracting parties may require that the contract be cancelled or terminated, whichever the case may be (893 UAE).

  If the contractor commences to perform the work and then becomes incapable of completing it for a cause in which he played no part, he shall be entitled to the value of the work which he has completed and the expenses he has incurred in the performance thereof up to the amount of the benefit the employer has derived there from (894 UAE).

  Under article 664 of the Egyptian law and 685 of the Kuwaiti law, the contract will be terminated for the impossibility of the contract subject matter. Article 663 of the Egyptian law allows the employer to terminate the contract for convenience and stop the execution of work any time before its completion upon his discretion, provided he compensates the contractor for what he has spent, the work performed, and all he would have gained had the work been completed.

The court may reduce the loss of profit compensation due to the contractor, if the circumstances make this reduction fair. The court particularly must reduce the compensation an amount equal to what he has saved as a result of the contract termination by the employer, and equal to what he has gained as a result of using his time and resources in different activities.

Contracting Process for Turnkey Projects

Building an integrated information system for an institution can be similar to the construction of a building or a residential complex as such projects need several types of experience, whether in design, assembly, development, execution, finishing, or delivery. In the construction industry, for example, there are architectural, constructional, electrical, sanitary, air conditioning-related matters, etc. In the information system projects, there are numerous elements involved, such as computer hardware, software, networks, multiple services, and many sorts of specializations and project-management experiences. Companies working in this field bear the major risks and responsibilities, as they are solely accountable to the customer for design, supply, installation, customization, integration, warranty, and interconnections between the components of the system as well as other systems during and after execution. They must be able to deal with different suppliers, link scattered parts of the system and deliver all together to the customer, as one integrated unit, at the agreed cost and within the scheduled time. All parts of the system must work in harmony and efficiently in accordance with the agreed specifications.

It varies from one project to another according to a number of factors, including the type and nature of the information system, scope of project, project size, value, time, complexity, size of organization, industry, data, technology, etc. However, as related to this study, we can identify *four main stages,* as simplified in the table below, each of which raises a number of risks.

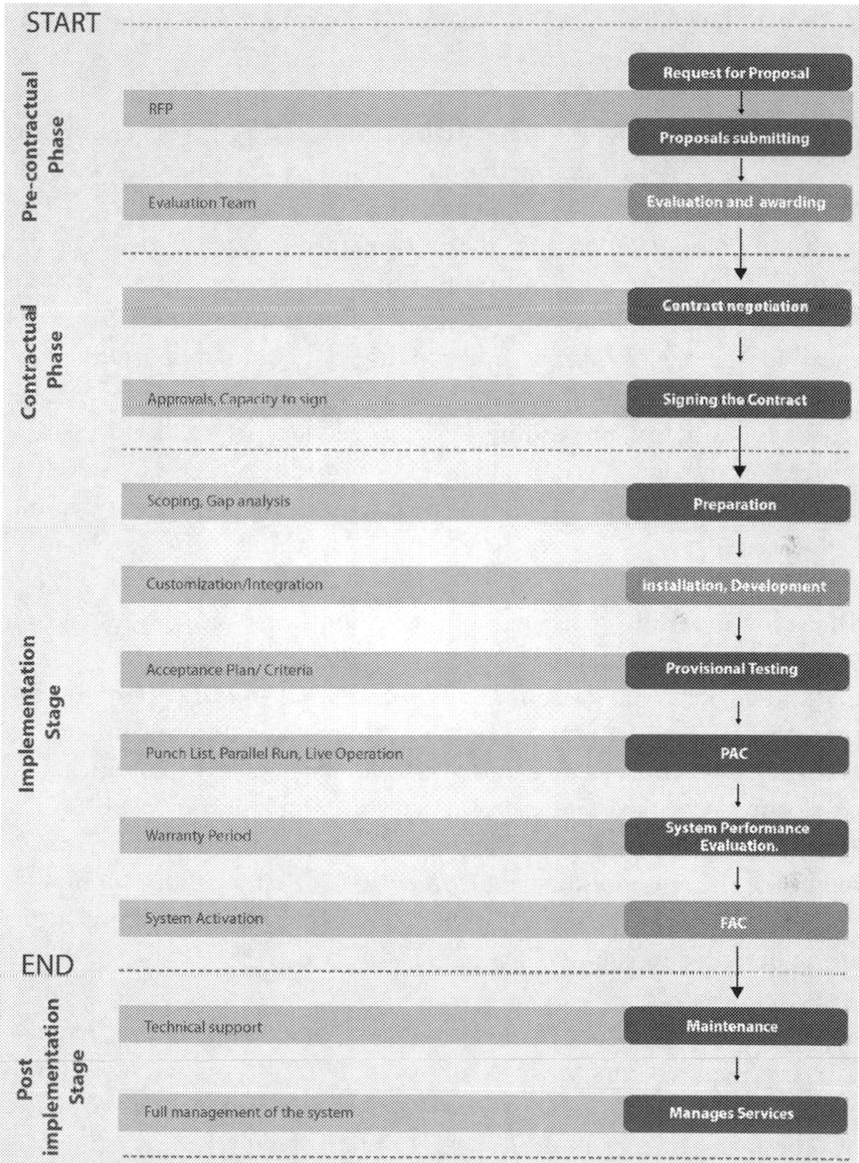

Figure 6: Contracting Process for a Turnkey Project

Pre-Contracting Stage: At this stage, the nature of the required information system is precisely determined through an analytical study. The determination of the proposed system may be carried out by experts, specialized in this field from the customer staff or to be performed by an independent external consultant if the customer lacks the necessary experience.

Key Point: We would like to highlight the importance of being cautious and precise while selecting the entity that will prepare this study, since the findings that will come up will have a great impact on the organization. This is because the information system to be chosen is required to perform a major function in the organization. This system is also supposed to be adopted by the organization for many long years ahead to manage its business and activities. The most important factor for the entity which is to be entrusted to select the information system is its profound understanding and knowledge of the nature of the business of the organization and its current and future needs, as well as the organization's ability to use the new system. Also, this entity should be impartial.

The study must include, among other things, an accurate description of the current information system, if any (its hardware, software, and methodologies), the technical and functional specifications of the proposed system, the relations between the current system components and the new proposed one and available alternatives, the anticipated cost or the proposed budget for execution, and the time expected for execution. After finalizing the study and preparing comprehensive reports of the study results, a document titled "request for proposal" is prepared based on the results of the study, after which the competitors are to be called to submit their offers.

Suppliers work together in this phase for responding to that request. They sign agreements that initially provide the terms and conditions governing their commercial relations and teaming up during the phases of submitting offers and project execution, if they were selected.

Competing suppliers submit their technical and financial proposals to provide the system in response to the said request. At this stage, the proposals will be evaluated by examining their compliance with the requirements and standards specified in the` request for proposal document, and then the successful competitor will be selected.

The underlying risk factor here is that the key business requirements and main features of the system become crystallized at this stage. Any misunderstanding or misconception sows a seed for failure. That is why it is urged by the experts to make such requirements and features clear to the vendors in the invitation to bid. The invited vendors are also supposed to explore and gather the actual and correct requirements and analyse such requirements as well.

***Key Point*:** Here we would like to stress the indispensability of being careful in selecting the entity and the team that will evaluate the proposals, and an absolute necessity of that team being equipped with a rich knowledge and impartiality. Criteria for vendor selection may include cost of system implementation, time of implementation, track record and references, resources availability, financial insolvency, etc.

Contracting Stage.[75] This stage comes immediately after awarding the project to the winning competitor, and when certain activity starts with the winner to agree on the terms and conditions which will be the overall frame of the project. We identify two main activities at this stage that parties should perform with utmost care and attention:

a. The parties negotiate and agree on all the relevant terms and conditions related to the project.
b. They formulate precisely and accurately what has been agreed to in a state-of-the-art document called a contract. Here we would like to reiterate that this document is a crucial tool which can be used effectively to manage the risks associated with the turnkey projects. The underlying analysis of this book is based on the contentment that this stage is central and holds a vital significance for project success which has been overlooked by most of the researchers.

Execution Stage: After signing the contract, and after a short mobilization period, the contract goes to the implementation stage, where it passes through some stages that are documented in detail in the scope of work, implementation plan, and other documents attached to

---

75 Chapter 6 is sololy dedicated to providing specific guidances and pertinent recommendations on how to deal with the activities of this stage.

the contract. Following are some major activities in the implementation phase (see also the figure at the end of this chapter for more information).

- **Delivery:** Delivery here means the material delivery (i.e. physical handing over of the system components, such as the hardware and media in which the software is loaded). This delivery should be done at the agreed place and time and according to the normal process, namely using a delivery note[76]. Delivery is a mere initial step that has no legal value in relation to the acceptance or completion of the information system itself. However, the main arguable issue at the time is, who will be responsible for safeguarding the parts and components delivered to the customer from the date of material delivery?[77]
- The site preparation, where the hardware will be installed in terms of construction, electricity, connections, and cable extensions, is the responsibility of the customer and should be performed according to the agreed schedule so that the supplier is not held accountable for any delay on the part of the customer. The customer may, before preparing the site, request from the supplier, and the required technical specifications for that preparation. The preliminary and final delivery of the system is to be addressed later in this chapter.
- **System Implementation:** This being the core activity of turnkey projects, it consumes most of the project time. At this stage, the supplier starts building and developing, installing and commissioning the system. This includes installing the software application on the equipment prepared for this purpose, and developing, customizing, and adjusting the software to match the technical specifications and desired functionalities. This stage is carried out in close cooperation with the team appointed by the customer.

  In this phase, the actual activities of replacing the legacy system (or having a Greenfield system) start. Presumably, at the end of this, the customer should have a new system running properly. For each implementation, there will be an *implementation planning* phase that starts with drawing a high level implementation strategy and then drawing a frame of work

76 Delivery note is an evidance document that the products has been delivered,

77 Related to this point, see "Title and Risk" in this chapter.

and finally, step by step (tasks and milestones) on the basis of what will be done and how it will be done, deliverables which will be produced at each step. These steps start usually with the projects kick-off and end with system activation. The project management approach will definitely be a significant part of such strategic planning. A comprehensive implementation plan and an implementation methodology will be the first deliverable produced at the time of or before signing the contract. It is said, "each implementation is different if not unique, perhaps there is no typical and identical implementation".[78]

The following is a specimen of a major milestone of an implementation structure in an IT turnkey system project:

- requirements gathering
- implementation planning
- off-site implementation
- onsite implementation
- activation of the system

Such milestone can be viewed from a slightly different perspective, as follows:

- project planning
- system design
- system implementation
- system activation

The above major phases are divided into *sub-phases* and tasks, whereas each task demands for the qualified and skilled resources, time for completion, and cost. A number of documents are expected to be produced during the implementation phase such as scoping documents, configuration document, implementation approach document, and configured products. *Documentation* and reporting of every step during the implementation are very important for knowledge transfer and in case one of the key team members leaves the company. Undoubtedly, a comprehensive documentation is a crucial factor for project success.

78 Phil Simon, Op, Cite, 312.

Meanwhile, the lack of proper documentation plants another seed of project failure.

As mentioned above, each task requires *qualified resources*, as the lack of skilled resources from both parties (since the implementation is a shared responsibility between supplier and customer) during the implementation is another seed for project failure. A backup plan must be in place in case one of the resources decides to leave during the implementation.

One of the most important tasks during the implementation of the system is the *gap analysis*. The purpose of this task is to identify and highlight the gaps (or differences) between the proposed system and the client's business requirements. It also relates to what is called an application exploration, where the parties work together to explore the features and functions of the new system.

Testing: This phase incorporates the tests performed from time to time during the implementation and system development phase, to ensure that the system or some parts of it are performing the desired functions according to the agreed specifications. Moreover, this phase identifies the issues that may need to be fixed or adjusted, whether related to the system configuration, data migration, data entry, or any other. Depending on the severity of the issues discovered, the system will be considered succeed or fail to pass the acceptance test. There will be several types of tests according to the system type or size, such as the installation test, integration test, functional and non-functional acceptance test, user acceptance test (UAT), and system performance evaluation test (SPET). We will discuss acceptance tests later in this chapter.

Acceptance: Acceptance of the system occurs when the system *passes all the agreed tests* and meets all the agreed standards. It is supposed (if all goes well) that tests end at the stage where the system is able to satisfy all the agreed requirements and fulfils the required functionalities as of the agreed specifications. At this point, the system supposedly is ready to start live operation (i.e. to perform data processing and fulfil the required and planned functions of a live environment).

However, the decision to start the *live operation* is up to the customer, for the important implications it carries. The system reaches this phase just after successfully passing the test. At this point, the customer should immediately issue a certificate called a provisional acceptance certificate, which means the system has successfully passed the tests and is ready for live operation. This certificate stipulates that the system has mainly passed the acceptance tests.

However, there will always be some *minor concerns* or errors, which do not hinder the system from performing the main functions. Such concerns and errors are put on a list (sometimes called a punch list) to be attached to the provisional acceptance certificate. Some simple and minor errors do not mean the system has failed to pass the tests an accurate definition of such errors and comments should be set forth and agreed upon in advance in order not to be disputable.

The contract should regulate the case where the system has successfully passed the acceptance tests as agreed but the customer refuses to issue the acceptance certificate. In such a case, the contract should consider that the system has passed the test so it is legally "*deemed accepted*" after notifying the customer of the evidence and a specified period of time (say seven days), indicating the implications for the acceptance of the system. The system can also be deemed to be legally accepted when the customer starts live operation before (or after) the acceptance tests have been conducted, whether or not the customer has issued the certificate.

The contract should also address the case(s) when *the system fails to pass the acceptance testing* after a certain number of attempts. In such a case, all the system deviations from the agreed specifications and levels of performance should be documented. The contract should also specify the maximum number of times allowed for conducting the acceptance tests (e.g. three times), after which the customer may terminate the contract and claim for all consequences accordingly.

Warranty Period: The warranty period usually *starts when the contractor fulfills his commitments* and obligations related to the implementation of the project, which will be confirmed by the issuance of the provisional acceptance certificate (PAC). The main obligation of the contractor during this period (that may last between three months to one year more or less from the date of issuance of the certificate) is to ensure the system as a whole is working in an integrated and harmonious manner, whether internally or with other systems of the customer, as was agreed in the beginning.

The contractor is committed during the warranty period to *fix any errors* that may appear in relation to the integration of the system. This means there can be different warranty periods for the parts of the system, separately. There may be, for example, a three or six month warranty period for the software applications, and another period for the hardware that starts and ends on different dates. Such different periods are important in relation to the beginning of the paid maintenance periods, as such maintenance period starts once the warranty periods end, given that this does not prejudice the main obligation of the contractor; that is to say it warrants the system as a whole for a certain period of time.

Some parties prefer to put the system (whether it commences the commercial services or not) under what is called a *system performance evaluation* (SPE) for a certain period of time (usually ninety days or more). The objective of this evaluation is to ensure that the system operates in a live environment or simulated one in accordance with the requirements of this type of evaluation. Such requirements must be agreed between parties in advance.

In case there are third parties' products, the contract must specify clearly the *warranty given by third parties* directly to the customer. During the warranty period, the contractor commits to solve minor problems and errors that appeared during the provisional acceptance tests, that do not hinder the live performance of the system as a whole and that the contractor committed to make right during the warranty period.

Completion of the Project *(the Mission Impossible)***:** This is one of the puzzles and distressful dilemmas in the turnkey projects, in which the most elusory question is: When is the project/contract finally completed and closed. Basically the project/contract, in an ideal scenario, will be considered accomplished when everything goes as planned (i.e. the system has been delivered, designed, configured, developed, tested, operated, and warranted successfully on time, and no conflict arises at any stage about any of the project aspects except minor issues which can be tolerated).

Once the warranty period ends and the supplier has fulfilled the rest of his obligations, such as training, delivering documents, and solving the problems listed in the acceptance certificate, the supplier is deemed to have fulfilled his obligations and the project is considered completed. Article 892-896 of the UAE civil code provided that "the contract [Muqawala] will be expired upon the completion of the work subject to the contract". The question still remains of *when in actual the work is considered completed.* The two parties may agree to issue a final acceptance certificate, which means the completion of the project and release of the supplier from any obligations other than such obligations which will, as stated in the contract, continue in effect even after the contract term ends. From a contractual standpoint, the contract will be expired and the project will be completed upon the occurrence of the following:

- The contractor receiving the acceptance certificates (PAC and FAC).
- The system operation during the warranty period is in accordance with system specifications or the SPE.
- The client has received all the documentations and training from the contractor.

Upon the occurrence of the above, the contract will be deemed expired, the project will be deemed complete and the contractor will be considered fulfilled his obligations under the contract and will not be under any obligation except those survived any termination.

A Point to Ponder

The above scenario presents an ideal situation that the contracting parties dream about. Unfortunately, the implementation of IT projects is not always the case, as on the other extreme, the project may be declared a failure and the contract is terminated in the middle of nowhere. In between the above two scenarios is *a wide range of grey scenarios,* including delay in completion of the project due to scope; at the time of completion a few of the system functions are satisfied, the system has been completed on time or with minor delay, but with a lot of errors and bugs. Since most of the parties experience these "in-between scenarios", it becomes arduous to answer the question of when the system is finally completed. The situation will be more complicated when the dispute arises between the parties around who is responsible for the delay and deviation from the agreed functionalities in an endless vicious circle.

Post-Execution Phase: this phase starts when the system goes into commercial operation. The successful operation of the system depends, to a large degree, on what has been planned for during the previous stages. Planning for this phase is as important as any other phase, and the contract can still play a significant role if the drafter can understand and predict the requirements of this phase. Examples of this is the documentation (prepared during the contracting and execution phase), which will help the users to operate and maintain the system; training and preparation of the skilled users including backup and succession planning. Another dimension is the preparation and planning for system expansion and upgrade, maintaining the system, and system management.

Construction of a Turnkey Contract

Chapter 4 dealt with the construction of IT contracts in general, where we classified the provisions of software and IT contracts into three categories: core, general, and standard. Same classification applies to the construction of turnkey provisions, as follows:

Core Provisions	• Scope of the contract • Specifications • Contract duration • Related provisions: • Schedules • Changes control • Implementation plan • Acceptance

General Provisions	• Form of contract • Definitions • Contractual documents • Parties to the contract • Recital • Contract value • Risk and title • Warranties • IPRs • Delay & liquidated damages • Liability • Termination • Governing law • Settlement of disputes
Standard Provisions	• Force majeure • Notices • Confidentiality • Assignment • No waiver • No solicitation • Severability • Entire agreement • Originals of agreement

Table 8: Construction of Turnkey Provision

Core Provisions: When reduced to its essentials, the turnkey project will be stigmatized as "failed" in the following events:

- if the scope of the contract is not achieved totally or partially
- the scope of the contract is achieved but too late due to scope creep, data issue, lack of enough or skilled resources, lack of sincere cooperation between parties, or any other reason
- achieved with only a few operating functions, along with errors and bugs

Based on the above, the core provisions of turnkey project can be identified from the perspective of the project failure events (along with their related provisions) as follows:

- o scope of contract

- o system specifications
- o project duration

Adhering your focus on the above-mentioned areas during the contracting phase will help manage the risks associated with turnkey projects.

General Provisions: These provisions incorporate the backbone terms and conditions of turnkey contracts and other IT contracts. Being a mainstay, these provisions have been addressed, analysed, and examined from the following perspectives:

- the classification of IT contract provisions "core", "general", and "standard housekeeping".
- the risk and exposure associated with each.
- the legal principals and doctrines as set forth in the ME legal system.

Standard provisions: They have been addressed in Chapter 4 briefly, no point to repeat it here.

Note: Despite the fact that the core provisions Being the root of the contract and fundamental in a project's success, nothing here says any article is less important than another; all are crucial in the construction of a turnkey contract. Nothing here says core provisions can be seen separately. *All contract provisions are extensively interrelated and cross-referenced.* What we have intended solely is to *guide the parties about how the contract is structured and the effect of each on achieving the overall target.* For that, we will treat the provisions in a chronological manner as that of formal practice.

Contract Form

The provisions that we shall note here assume that the appropriate contract form has been selected, since software and IT contracts differ from other industries'. In fact, within the realm of the software industry, the forms of contractual agreement vary with the numerous activities, products, and services. The form of contract represents a specific business transaction. As such, a form of contract for selling the software will vary from the form of licensing the same software. Likewise, a form for designing and implementing a turnkey IT project differs from that involving the provisioning of professional consultation services.

IT Contract forms differ significantly. IT outsourcing differ from turnkey, and a software maintenance contract varies from a software development one. Moreover, the forms within the same category differ considerably. For instance, inside the license category you will find wildly different forms[79]. While on the other hand, forms drafted from a supplier perspective will definitely differ from the one drafted by the customer. Therefore, a scrupulous attention must be given in order that the most appropriate contract format for the project at hand is used.

Definitions

We had been laying an utmost emphasis on the significance of the clarity and accuracy of contract provisions and clauses in the previous chapters, in such a way that is necessary to avoid any possible perplexity, misunderstanding or misinterpretation; otherwise they would constitute a source of risk. The parties must ensure an intensified accurate use of words and phrases. Therefore, we find that the introduction or preface of most contracts comprises of a set of definitions utilized throughout the document and the meaning or connotation of each. The definition of the technical terms used in the contract is very important to remove misunderstanding, not only among the technical and business personnel of both parties but also for judges and arbitrators and any 3rd party. This clause also serves the purpose of shortening phrases or introducing acronyms so that full phrases are not repeated incessantly.

Contract Documents

Throughout this book, the significance of documenting processes of all documents produced has been strongly emphasized. This should be done during pre-contractual, contractual, and contract implementation

[79] See table 7 in Chapter 4.

phases. The lack of documented reports, interfaces, system configuration, test results, training materials, user manuals, and so on can have a severe impact not only on the parties in case of disputes but on the success and failure of the project and the use of the system after the system activation.

In turnkey projects, the contract is comprised of several documents, including the main body of the contract, annexes, and other related documents the party may wish to make part of the contract, such as the proposal, MOU, POs, and NDA, Teaming Agreements, Sub Contracts, all of which constitute the contract. The contract must be marshalled in the precedence of such documents in case of any inconsistency between them, usually in the same order as they are listed. Annexes, appendixes, and schedules attached to the contract often pertain to the more technical and commercial aspects of the projects. They are extremely important since they exhibit the most critical components of the project, including the scope and details of the system, system specifications, acceptance plan and criteria, integration services, price list, time schedule, and many others. A negotiation team must ensure that schedules have been duly reviewed and signed by the concerned technical teams. Any amendments to the schedules must be reviewed and signed by the concerned teams. Before the project starts, the project manager and his team must get the full set of contractual documents.

Recital

The preface, or "recital", or "whereas clause", is a short summary depicting the nature and subject of the contract, and intends to clarify the circumstances and reasons for signing the contract using brief and simple language. In formulating the recital, the drafter should be well educated about project details, the nature of the relationship binding the parties hereto, the primary products and services involved, and so forth. Some trends involve formulating the recital in a detailed and meticulous manner, so it extensively describes the motives and circumstances of the contract. This is to ensure that the implementing party (the vendor) is aware of all conditions and circumstances surrounding the contract and that it fully appreciates the critical and sensitive nature of the project at hand. Moreover, it has the necessary technical, financial, and human skilled resources required for completing the project.

There is no harm in having an elaborate and detailed preface, although a brief, succinct account is preferable – one that refers to the proposal submitted by the implementing party, or the license obtained by the project owner, for instance. The recital must also outline the relationship between the parties, especially if the contractual relationship is a complex and interrelated one, such as one party signing the contract on behalf of another party (for whatever reason), or if the signing party is the mother company of an affiliate, etc. Reference should also be made to whether the provider has other partners involved in providing the products and services mentioned in the contract, together with the nature of their relationship. On the other hand, the parties should pay attention to the warranties and representations usually given the recital, since the recital is sometimes used to introduce warranties and representations.

Scope of Contract

In my view, this element is the main source of risk in turnkey projects, and being the core of the turnkey contract, outlining the products and services upon which the contract is founded, and is what gives the contract its substance. The scope of the contract (or project) basically answers the following questions:

- i- What exactly is the description of the system that will be delivered?
- ii- How it will be delivered?
- iii- What will the system do after activation?
- iv- What are the services associated and specific deliverables?

The scope of the turnkey contract usually addresses the following elements:

- description of the system in whole, including system components (software and hardware), system design, and how it will be composed

- installation and commissioning of the system, including integration services
- system specifications and functionality
- testing of the various components of the system to ensure compliance with system specifications; integration and interoperability of the system with other external systems in accordance with the system specifications
- support services to the system defects during the warranty and after the activation of the system
- scheduling and the delivery of the above
- obligations and responsibilities of each party during project implementation in each and every phase thereof (where possible), excluded products and services not part of the system that could cause confusion and disputes if not included
- contract disengagement services in case project enters into a serious turbulent contract termination

It is customary for the provider, based on customer requirements, to submit a "scope of work" statement that scrupulously details the items and activities included within the scope of project implementation phases, and whether the project entails one or more stages. The provider should also list the project deliverables through a "scope of delivery" document and the project management methodology. He should identify:

- the "project planning" approach,
- the business requirement definition,
- solution design, and
- how he will implement the system.

The project activities should be detailed in the form of an "implementation plan"; that is, how that provider will perform the system acceptance. The document should be detailed enough to specify whether provider responsibilities include data migration from an old system to the new one or any other relevant activity such as data extraction and cleansing, and data construction prior to migration. Moreover, the training program proposed by the supplier, scope of integration of system components, quality assurance conditions, and the way and procedures the system will be handed over to the customer (roll out) at the completion date together with anticipated operation and maintenance are the elements that must be specified as well. The document later on will be treated as the constitution of the project.

A more clear and specific formulation of project scope will result in the following important consequences:

a. Any other item and activities will be impliedly excluded.[80]
b. That being any modification, request, or addition to the scope of work shall be considered a "change request", warranting specific procedures as outlined by the "change control" clause.

From the legal standpoint, this element is one of the mandatory elements to design a contract. As per the law of contract terminology, this is the "contract subject matter". The UAE civil code (article 129) provides: "The subject matter of the contract must be something which is possible and defined or capable of being defined and possible to be dealt in". In fact, if the scope of the contract is not well defined, it might cause the contract to be null and void or at least might cause a confusion and lead to dispute.

Article 874 of the UAE law provides: "In a Muqawala contract, there must be a description of the subject matter of the contract, and particulars must be given to the type and amount thereof, the manner of performance, and the period over which it is to be performed, and the consideration must be specified".

Article 141 of the UAE civil code provides almost the same language of article 95 of the Egyptian civil code): "(1) a contract may only be made upon the agreement of the two parties to the essential elements of the obligation, and the other lawful conditions which the parties regard as essential. (2) if the parties agree on the essential elements of the obligation and the remainder of the lawful conditions which both parties regard as essential, and they leave matters of detail to be agreed upon afterwards but they do not stipulate that the contract

80 Except items necessary for the completion of the project (requirements and appurtenant) under article 246/2 UAE law and148/1 Egyptian law.

shall not be regarded as made in the event of absence of agreement upon such matters which have not been agreed upon, the judge shall adjudicate thereon in accordance with the nature of the transaction and the provision of law."

This simply command the parties to put the scope of the project at the top of their priority. When they do so, the scope must be clear and well defined, otherwise the door will be opened for disputes. Furthermore, the whole contract might be in jeopardy. Finally, when talking about the scope of the project, it is worth noting that a great part of provider liability arises from this area (the scope of the project) as a result of one or all of the following:

a. provider not performed the scope entirely or partially
b. delay in delivery or completion of one of the activities as stated in the scope document
c. The provider performed his obligations but with defects in the system

Contract/Project Duration

This refers to the time period required for implementing the project or contract validity period. In general, the time frame varies from one IT contract to another. In turnkey or system procurement projects, contract duration may correspond with the project implementation period or could be a longer period than project implementation (see figures 7 and 8 below). Contract duration may also be determined by a specific time frame (months or years) while being automatically extendable or by agreement of both parties, as with contracts involving software distribution and marketing, software maintenance and technical support, and software development. They may also be of unspecified duration, as in software licensing agreements, where the licensee supposedly requests a perpetual license for software use.

In some cases, a contract may initially begin with a specific preliminary duration (one year, for instance), thereafter transforming to a contract of indefinite duration, with an automatic renew for equal intervals (normally annually), unless either party informs the other party of its wish not to renew for a certain period of time in advance of the annual renewal date. This is usually the case with contracts pertaining to services, distribution, and marketing.

In the definite contracts, the duration is usually one year, whereas in some contracts requiring substantial investment on the part of the supplier – as in IT outsourcing contracts – the required duration can be relatively long (three years, for instance), so that the supplier can benefit from the return on investment (ROI) as long as he is performing all his obligations. In all cases, the contract's effective date must be accurately specified. The contract's effective date is the one in which the contract will come into force and effect. It can be specified by a date (such as the contract signing date), event, or condition (such as board approval or the client grant license to operate a mobile system). Project schedule or project implantation plan (that is, the period of time planned to accomplish the project) is also quite relative to the contract duration, since it entails distribution of the tasks, activities, and services throughout the contract duration until the final delivery. Project duration is divided into phases or milestones, each having distinct natures, products, and maybe even specific schedules. The project schedule commands special significance due to its association with payments, liabilities, penalties, and so forth. However, the implementation plan is not limited to project services or schedule, but also comprises what is called a "responsibility matrix", which is a table defining the responsibilities and obligations of each party during project execution. The plan calls for both parties to commit to all stated dates, duties, and responsibilities, otherwise they would be in violation of their contractual obligations.

It is worthy to be noted here that contract duration may expire, yet some of the contract obligations survive such expiration (i.e. remain in effect), such as the confidentiality obligation and other obligations pertaining to warranty. The delay in completion of turnkey projects is also related to the project duration. Any deviation from the agreed time of delivery or completion will be considered a default which may trigger the contractual liability and the application of the liquidated damages.

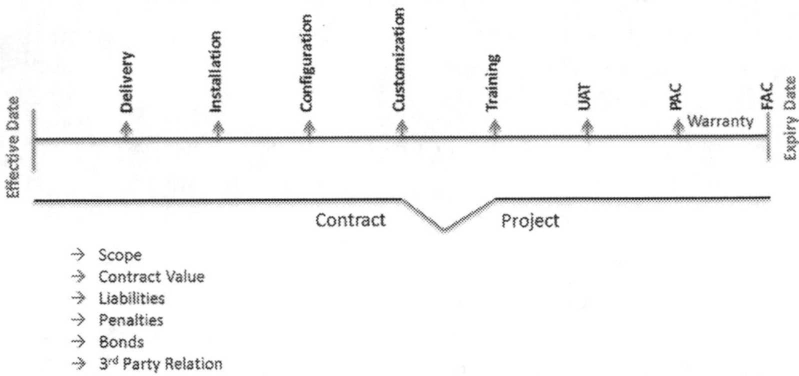

Figure 7: *This figure (7) outlines the relationship between the project and the contract on one hand, and the matching of the durations on the other. We see that project duration corresponds to contract duration; starting and ending together, where the contract works to outline the agreed terms and conditions between the parties for executing the project. The above figure also highlights the theory on which this book is based, that a contract may greatly contribute to reducing the failure rate afflicting IT projects and mitigating the risks present in this industry, if it is formulated in a way that is efficient and impartial.*

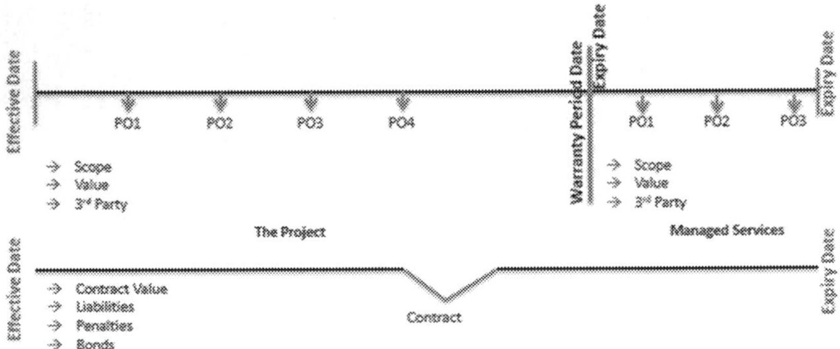

Figure 8: Contract/project Duration.

This figure (8) sketches a slightly different picture, where contract duration extends beyond the project implementation period to the following phase;

which is the maintenance and technical support or managed services. In this instance, the contract is instilled with special terms and clauses pertaining to project implementation, in addition to the special conditions associated with Managed Services (the phase in which the system is managed, operated and maintained).

Contract Value

This corresponds to the financial aspects of the project, the charges, consideration, or payment affected to the party provisioning the products or services during contract duration. Clauses pertaining to financial matters are generally of high interest to both contracting parties, as it is important for the customer to be aware of his expenditure in return for the products and services rendered, while the supplier is interested in determining his profit from the deal. The provisions associated with a contract value raise a number of issues, some of which we outline here:

- Is the value a fixed and predetermined sum? Is it based on the time and materials spent? Is it a net amount, or would it warrant adding transport charges, insurance fees, shipping and clearance expenses, etc.? Which party shall bear government fees and taxes, if any? Are there any bank guarantees or letters of credit involved, and will a specific amount be withheld for payment against completion or delivery? How will payment instalments be made (by cheque, bank transfer, etc.)? Is interest being imposed on delayed payments?
  In the case of ongoing supply contracts, the charges and payment provisions must regulate the issue of price increase or decrease, while it is also possible to include special agreements pertaining to currency fluctuations and which – perhaps both – party shall be expected to bear them, after having agreed on an exchange rate.
- The provisions must also regulate the matters related to other costs and expenditures, such as travel and accommodation expenses of the supplier's team, the limit incurred for such expenses, the means for demanding payment, and their supporting documents.

- Also, it is important to include an explicit statement regarding payment terms. Should instalments be connected to a specific milestone or to any phase of implementation, this must be clearly stated, for it is inadequate to mention that the payment is due against "delivery" if it is not properly or accurately defined. There is no reason for the client to withhold payments whenever they are due, except if and when the supplier has violated or failed to undertake any of the duties and obligations in delivering, installing, or handing over the product or service. More often than not the advance payment is guaranteed by a letter of credit (LC). Finally, the provisions must also go on to explain the payment and invoicing mechanism.
- It is to be noted that in turnkey contracts (Muqawala), the general rule is: if the prices of the raw materials, labour and other costs increase, the contractor is not allowed to ask for an increase of the contract price, even if such increase (in materials and labour) is high to an extent that it makes the execution of the contract difficult (658/3 Egypt).
- However, If the economic balance between the obligations of the contractor and the employer collapse as a reason of general exceptional accidents which were unforeseen at the time of signing the contract, and such accidents result in the collapse of the basis on which the Muqawala contract was established, the judge may increase the contract consideration or adjudicate the rescission of the contract (658/4 Egypt).

Specifications

The specifications of the software or the system constitute one of the most important components of the turnkey projects, and accordingly a "core provision", if not the most significant one. This is because the specifications are in fact the heart of the system to be developed, and a prime source of risk, due to the following reasons:

1. The specifications are directly related to the essence of the development process, since they are relevant to the functionality,

what is expected of it (functions), and how the system is set or configured to perform these functions (speed and quality).

2. The specifications lay down the foundations upon which software performance is measured, hence very crucial and decisive in case of dispute.
3. They are a prime source of risk in software and IT industry, since the inaccuracy of specifications leads to the rise of changing requests – and hence delay increased costs, the likeliness of disputes and so forth – culminating in failure.
4. The specifications itself can be used as a major and significant criteria to measure the performance of the system in achieving the agreed results and functionality.

With that said, at the very least the specification document must cover four principle points:

1. the number and quantity of software applications to be developed as accurately as possible
2. an accurate description of the required functions of the software
3. description of the hardware on which the software will operate
4. the speed and competency with which such system functions will be performed

In order to devise this description, the client must respond to the following questions from a practical perspective in relation to his day-to-day activities: Why is the system required? What are the functions sought to be performed by the system? What are the problems that would be solved by the new system? What impact does the system have on business growth and competitive advantage?

It is therefore imperative, prior to entering into a turnkey agreement, to accurately outline the technical specifications, functional specifications, data, information, and other details requested from the client. In some cases (such as in software development), the parties may agree on the high-level specifications and leave the detailed specification task to be undertaken by the parties following contract agreement during a specific duration from the date of contract signature, and in accordance with a "scoping study" of client needs. The parties must spare no effort in documenting these specifications in detail as accurately as possible.

The whole process goes through a number of phases, whereby the first stage involves the compilation of a "requirements-specification document", which is a business document articulating, in simple language, the demands of the client and the parties' vision of the intended system. Based on this document, the "system-design document" is prepared, which is a technical document where the developer sets forth his accurate visualization for converting customer requirements to actual designs and technical specifications describing the system function. Once this document is approved, the contractor starts the development process, which is accompanied by software testing at every step. We note here and as previously indicated that any fundamental modification to software specifications shall be considered a change request and thus will lead to the following:

- (i) the necessity of obtaining the other party's approval for making the desired changes
- (ii) the entitlement of the contractor to demand additional fees and time for implementing these modifications. And since the modifications requested during project implementation are considered a source of risk, we therefore advise both parties to be careful with it and must agree upon a specific mechanism pertaining to change requests, and to detail the same in the contract agreement.

Key Point: The system specification is very important from other prospect as well; as it determines whether the software is defected or not. So accordingly, it determines whether there is a breach of contract or not. The point has been recognized in 2003 in the English courts as *Co-operative Group (CWS) Ltd. v International Computers Limited*, which in principal applies to the ME (Middle East) legal system. The court said, "A bug, when reduced to its essentials, [is] a respect in which software does not perform as expected. In considering what was expected, one has to have regard to what was specified as the functionality to be provided. Vagueness of the wording of the relevant specifications, the first area in which different assessors may reach different conclusions as to whether a supposed bug really is a bug or not. A conclusion that what it is said the software should do was not covered by the specifications written could lead to the view either that what was complained of was not a bug at all, or that it was really a request for the software to be modified to provide a different functionality – in other word, a change".[81] This shows, on the other hand, how important is to draft the specifications and to express them in an explicit and accurate manner.

Change Control

Orders presented by one of the parties (especially the client) following contract signature and during project implementation are deemed as a request to amend what has been agreed before. It is in fact one of the culprits insofar as the failure of IT and software projects. In spite of the importance of availing an opportunity for carrying out some amendments on the technical aspects of the project that may sometimes be necessary, the frequent exaggeration of these amendments may lead to hindering project implementation and slowing down the execution rate. It is also possible for these changes to alter the original project altogether. In this regard, it is important to shed light on a few relevant points regarding this issue:

The amendments discussed here are often those pertaining to the project's technical specifications, products, services, or the technical aspects related to the overall scope of the project. The changes range from being simple (at times so simple they are only verbally requested) to the more complicated orders that perhaps cause a major alteration as far as project scope, objectives, and specifications. Regardless of the magnitude and extent of the requested change, it is imperative that both parties agree upon *the mechanisms* involving the submission of change orders and the impact of the same on the project. As for legal amendments affecting contract provisions, these are rarely requested during the term of the agreement and are often regulated by a provision in the contract, which is separate to the one governing technical change orders.

---

[81] Dian Rowland, Uta Kohl and Andrew Charlesworth, *Information Technology Law*, Op. Cite, 437.

The change orders submitted for a project can result in increasing or decreasing the scope of the contract, which would then reflect on numerous other aspects of the project. Examples of these include prices, contract duration, products and services, and the required resources. Change orders must be utilized in a highly cautious way and should not be resorted to unless necessary. Parties may consider other available options, otherwise change orders must be employed professionally. As such, they must observe all agreed terms, conditions, guidelines, and procedures while mitigating any possible negative repercussions on the project itself. Any change order must be executed in accordance with the measures and procedures stipulated by the contract, which must not permit one party to unilaterally impose the change on the other party.

Change orders may indeed constitute a real problem and a source of risk, as in the case of a customer coercing a supplier to accept any change order without a subsequent increase in execution cost, required time for implementation, or at only a very slight increase that is not commensurate with the magnitude of the changes required. In fact, the analysis of the change order itself may require time, effort, and cost, which would be considered tedious and strenuous and could hamper the supplier from executing the project within the specified time, cost, and with the expected quality.

Change orders are closely associated with the extent and strength of the relationship between the parties, since their cooperation and mutual understanding throughout the project greatly contribute to achieving the required objective. Still, the formation of a designated team of both parties assigned with the responsibility of reviewing and swiftly handing the change orders, while cautiously seeking alternative methods, is expected to greatly enhance that objective. Should the amendment to the project constitute a major material one, it must be presented before a steering committee, and in any case, both parties must resume project implementation until a decision is reached on the change order.

Supposedly, change orders and all relevant financial commitments arising from them are agreed upon between the parties. However, we notice that in government contracts, it is permissible for the government entity to initiate a change order directly. In the case of larger projects, it is possible to designate a sum fund or a portion of the project budget towards funding any change requests, even though the assigned amount may resolve the cost issue but not the additional time required to implement the request, or the implications involving, extending the execution period, the necessary human resources, the impact on the completion of works demanded by the customer, or project finalization and actual operation.

As for the procedures pertaining to change requests or orders, these should be meticulously detailed in the contract. Initially, one of the parties (usually the client) submits a request outlining the nature and purpose of the required change, while asking for the other party's feedback and opinion regarding the same within a specific time period. This is to be submitted via a report describing the potential repercussions of the required change on other aspects of the project, the additional cost and the expected timeframe for making such change.

Both parties then proceed to discuss the change in light of the available data and upon close examination of the change request. Should they agree on all the details pertaining to project execution and possible implications, that request would then be formulated into an appendix, attached to the original contract, and would be considered an integral part of the agreement. In case the parties fail to agree on the terms and conditions of the requested change, the contract must then contain a reasonable mechanism, such as to revert the dispute to an external expert – with the costs involved being borne by both parties. That expert party would then submit its technical report as to the feasibility of the requested change and its potential impact on all aspects of the project. The parties may agree to consider the expert's verdict to be a final and conclusive one, or else the dispute would be reverted to the entity having jurisdiction – as stipulated in the contract – to resolve any disputes arising between the parties.

It should be noticed that the above procedure assumes no default from one party. Where the change mandates as result of an error in the design (for example), the error correction will be corrected at cost and liabilities of party responsible for the design.

Finally, the fundamental legal rule in the ME legal system is that contract is the law of the contracting parties, and it cannot be revoked or amended except by agreement of both parties or for the reasons provided by law.

***Advice*:** The contracting parties should stay bound to their commitments unless a valid or sudden circumstance mandates a change to what has been originally agreed upon. Parties should limit the use of change orders to absolutely necessary situations. Neither party should force the other to accept a request for change, and if accepted it must be under fair and reasonable terms and conditions.

Title and Risk

This point exhibits one of the problematic issues, that a contract should answer the question of who will bear the risk of loss and damage of the products and deliverables prior delivery, and when the title of such products and deliverables will be transferred. In other words, who will bear the risk of goods prior to delivery to customer? Will it be the selling party (system provider in IT contracts), being still in possession of the goods? Or will it be borne by the buyer, who is the new owner, albeit not in actual possession yet and when the title will be transferred to the new owner? In this regard, there exist two schools of thought in national legislation: one that connects liability to ownership, so that once ownership of goods is transferred to a party, that party shall also bear liability of the same. The other links liability to delivery, so that liability is automatically transferred to the buyer with delivery. This is the same principle upon which article 437 of the Egyptian civil law and Article 632 of the UAE Law are founded. It states that: "In the event goods deteriorate prior to delivery at no fault of the seller, then the transaction shall be deemed obsolete and the buyer shall be reimbursed, unless the dwindling occurred after notifying the buyer of readiness of goods for delivery".

The same principle was also adopted by the United Nations Convention on Contracts for the international sale of goods (Vienna 1980). Without delving into extensive details, the following points related to IT contracts ought to be clarified:

I. The transference of ownership is not applicable to software, since ownership is not automatically transferred to the client on all IT projects. Instead, the end user will be licensed to use the software upon certain terms and conditions. However, the title of the tangible components should pass to the purchaser upon paying its price in full unless agreed otherwise between parties.
II. The parties often undertake to regulate this matter themselves as opposed to resorting to such legislation. The adoption of either school of thought is usually negotiable and is dictated by the party with the upper negotiation hand. But in IT projects practice, we are of the opinion that it is best if both parties agree that the transference of ownership (of hardware and some other deliverables) is considered done upon affecting complete payment of project value. Meanwhile, the responsibility of safeguarding the goods (hardware and software media) shall be borne by the client immediately upon delivery of the tangible products at the site against damage or theft. As for the acceptance of the IT system with its agreed functions, this is a separate issue dealt with by another section of the contract.
III. More often than not, the customer insists on having the responsibility of safeguarding tangible products covered by the contract (including media containing the software) transferred to him upon the system passing the acceptance tests (PATs) and not the date of actual delivery. The problem here is that no distinction is made between the tangible goods (whether media for software or hardware devices) and the information system itself. The responsibility for preserving the IT system transfers to the client upon provisional delivery; however, the risk of the tangible elements (including media and hardware) is passed to him upon actual delivery.
IV. In turnkey projects, it is important to differentiate between the material components of the IT system separately and the system itself as a standalone component, during project implementation or upon completion thereof. It is for the client to be held responsible for safeguarding the material components

once they are materially delivered or handed over, while also preserving the integrity of the entire IT system following provisional acceptance of the same. Today, the insurance companies cover this risk until the goods are received by the buyer, which mitigates it to a greater extent.

Intellectual Propert Rights

It is customary for software and IT contracts to be concerned with the issue of intellectual property, since software programs and other related services are intellectual assets and are of vital importance to the owners of these rights. The matter of intellectual property is usually handled from a variety of prospects. The **first** of which is confirming that the supplier does indeed own such rights over products, services or documents covered by the contract. If he already owns such rights prior to entering into the contract, then these rights (in any form, whether patents, copyrights, trademarks, trade secrets, etc.) shall remain property him, and will be used also in accordance with the terms and conditions of the license agreement attached to the contract.

The **second** approach is known as "infringement claims" (sometimes called an indemnification clause), which is essentially a guarantee provided by the supplier to the client that the software and related material do not in any way infringe on the intellectual property rights of a third party. The contract itself regulates all procedures that should be followed in the event a third party claims to the customer that the IT system or a part of it, provided by the provider party, infringes on its intellectual rights.

The **third** and the most critical point is determining who owns the software or any deliverables produced during the project whether in the form of new software, interface, or customization of existing programs. The rule of thumb here is that each party continues to claim ownership of software or other intellectual property rights that were owned by it prior to entering into the contractual agreement (sometimes called "before ground"). The conflict remains, though, over the software produced or developed after the contractual relationship and during the project (sometimes called "after ground"), which is indeed a critical issue having no clear-cut rules and are resolved through negotiation.

However, suppliers usually insist on keeping the ownership of any derivative work or additions to its proprietary software, while customers insist to keep the ownership of the software that has been developed from scratch during the project and paid for. The parties must not neglect this point as it definitely will create future disputes. This dilemma has been demonstrated in the figure below.

The **fourth** issue relates to the provisions concerned with the confidentiality of exchanged data and information before and during project implementation. The rule here is that all information and data of either party exchanged between the parties – relevant to the contract or the project – must remain confidential and must not be disclosed in any way without the prior consent of the other party. The recipient party also undertakes to safeguard confidential information and to exercise utmost diligence and caution for protecting the same, including taking the necessary precautions with employees exposed to such data. This provision also regulates the exceptions to confidentiality and imposes the durations by which parties are expected to refrain from disclosing propriety information after the conclusion of the contractual agreement.

***Key Note*:** Due to the importance of the IPRs, the provisions regulating IPRs issues continue in full effect and survive termination and expiry of the agreement or termination for any reason. Also, for the same reason, any infringement of the IPRs allows the other party to take any immediate action without waiting or following escalation procedures.

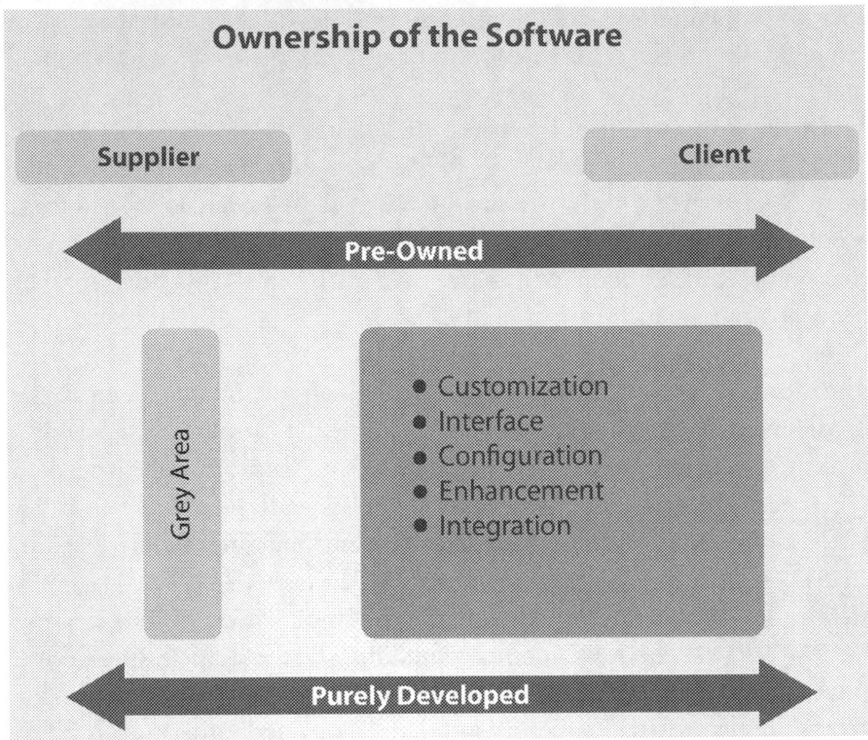

Figure 9: *This figure portrays ownership in the field of software projects, where this issue has been the nucleus of discussion and negotiation between the contracting parties. The general rule, as indicated by the figure, is that software owned by a party prior to the contract will remain so. The software developed or customized especially for the client at a charge, will (most often) be owned by the customer, or joint-ownership may be an option, on a case-by-case basis. The grey area in the middle represents the technologies and products created during the project implementation based on the customer specific requirements. This area usually creates potential disputes between contracting parties.*

Warranties and Representations

There are numerous warranties and representations given by and exchanged between parties in the contract. They include mainly two categories: one, the general warrantees given by one party to the other or in reciprocal basis, and two, warranties for products and services.

Examples under the first category include a warranty that the supplier is technically qualified to undertake the obligations and commitments stipulated by the contract, being legally competent to enter into a contractual relationship and capable of granting the other party a license for using the software and IT system, and that the regular use of the system shall not constitute an infringement of the intellectual property rights of any party. Product or service warranties include a guarantee that any equipment (if part of the contract) is new and has never been previously used, that this equipment is free of any visible, inherent, or unknown defects, it is not delivered as mortgaged, and the software (upon delivery) is free of any known viruses. We observe here that warranties for software do not include "error-free" warranties.

With regard to the products and services warranty, it mainly includes the ability of the software and IT system to operate properly during a specified time period (known as the free warranty period) and to efficiently perform their intended functions as per the agreed specifications, which must of course be documented in the contract schedules, and the system shall be free from any viruses, unauthorised codes, defective materials, or defective designs. Other products are licensed under the limited scope of warranty or limited periods. Associated with this type of warranty are the remedies and procedures that the supplier is expected to follow in order to remedy the breach of warranty or rectify any error occurring during the warranty period, whether by way of repair, correction, or replacement. Usually, the hardware and software manufacturers produce a separate document outlining the guarantees and warranties offered to all customers, including the remedies in case of breach of such warranties.

In turnkey contracts governing the delivery of IT turnkey systems, there are sometimes a number of specific warranties corresponding to the nature of such projects, most of which revolve around the quality and capacity of the system, such as the following:

a. Integration warranty, where the contractor warrants that the hardware and software shall perform and operate together as an integrated system
b. Capacity warranty, which refers to the capacity of the software and hardware ability to carry out the load of the business
c. Quality warranty, which means the system performance shall meet all quality parameters specified in the system specifications
d. Documentations, in which the contractor warrants that the documentation is free from any incorrect and/or omitted instructions and inaccuracies
e. Service warranty, in which the contractor warrants that the services provided during the project and warranty period will be carried out with due care and skill, in a professional manner and according to industry practices
f. Compatibility warranty, that the software and hardware all are compatible with system specifications, and any future expansion, enhancement, or correction.

Some software, especially mass-market and low-value software, is provided "as is", meaning with no warranty (probably except for the tangible media) and under the basis of "what you see is what you get". This is normally found in the US license agreements where it sets forth clearly that "the software, documentation, and all services provided hereunder are provided 'as is', with no warranty whatsoever. The licensor does not warrant that the functions contained in the software will meet the customer needs, or that the operation of the software will be uninterrupted or error free or that defects in the software will be corrected". The same concept is used in some limited cases with turnkey projects where the supplier is keen not to perform any customization during the implementation.

From the suppliers' perspective, they always try to limit the warranties and representations, especially with regard to the products and services during and after the project by limiting the scope of such warranties, including the period of the warranty, while the customer is trying to extend such warranties as much as they can. However, as I have always emphasized, it is crucial for both parties to create a fair and balanced contractual relationship. In this regard, other areas of the contract will be highly considered and synchronized while discussing the warranties and representations, such as the limitation of liability, indemnity, and insurance. In many cases, the suppliers will be reluctant to provide ongoing performance obligation for software lifetime.

In practice, the warranty period is usually perceived from the perspective of the project's components: hardware, software, services, third-party products and the like, and deal with each component separately. Moreover, in turnkey projects, there will be a warranty for the overall integrated system.

In most if not all IT contracts, the representations and warranties regarding the IPRs ownership and indemnification will be a major concern for the customer and will constitute an essential part of the discussion.

Finally, in some contracts, particularly the US style, the warranty clause is phrased as an "indemnity clause" and usually used in relation to losses arising through the breach of IPRs or trade secrets, and is often drafted without limits on the amount claimed by the beneficiary party. As noted by some writers[82], there is often confusion as to the role of an indemnity clause as opposed to a warranty clause. They noticed also that there is no reason why there should not be a limitation on the damage under the indemnity clause, just as there is a limitation of liability under the warranty clause. This type of warranty (IPRs) is covered in the ME legal system under what is called "not to challenge obligation" when the buyer warrants not to challenge or disturb the use of sold item by himself or by third party (article 439, Egyptian law).

Acceptance

An acceptance test is a key milestone in software and IT projects. It can be viewed as a central milestone as the results of which offers major proof whether the software can perform the agreed functions according to the agreed specifications. In turnkey projects, it provides major proof determining whether the system is ready to roll out into live

82 Software Contracts, Robert Bond, Op. Cite, 124

operation. In fact, it is also important evidence of the progress of the project implementation. This is because testing is an ongoing activity throughout the implementation cycle. The project team will execute many units and functional testing scenarios for every component and task. Obviously, the parties will not move to the next milestone unless the previous one passes the acceptance test.

At the end, the system will be deemed accepted only when the system passes all the agreed acceptance tests, which may include, for instance, in turnkey projects: preliminary acceptance tests (PATs), final acceptance test (FAT), system integration test, and live operation test. The acceptance plan and criteria usually drafted in a separate document are attached to the contract, which outline the criteria upon which the software, the system, or the services under the IT contract will be tested. The document covers the activities and obligations of both parties during the acceptance process, including the plan and procedures followed by both parties for testing the software or IT system, its components, parts, functions, relevant services, and the procedures should any defect occur during testing.

It includes also the criteria used during the testing. The objective of acceptance tests is to determine the readiness of the system, its capacity to process the data, and to achieve its targeted and agreed functions and duties through simulation of the real-life activities. Upon successfully completing acceptance tests, the customer issues a "provisional acceptance certificate", which is, in IT projects, a major milestone and vital document through which both parties confirm that the system has successfully passed the acceptance testing. It also verifies that the system is now in a position to go for live operation. The certificate proves that the supplier has successfully fulfilled the largest and most important part of his commitments and that the system is indeed ready for actual operation. Upon the issuance of this certificate, the supplier will be entitled to the related payment, and the warranty period will start; most importantly, the system in the integrated total solution will be under the responsibility of the provider from that time.

What remains for the provider are the undertakings imposed by the free warranty period (i.e. rectifying errors classified as "low" in the severity level [such as interface display, font size, position, colour] and are assumed not be the major ones, otherwise the system would not be operational emanating from the acceptance tests). It is important to mention here that the system's fulfilment of acceptance tests does not necessarily correspond to its error-free nature. There remains a need to address some minor flaws or errors. These are usually noted in a document signed by both parties, for rectification during the free warranty period, lasting anywhere from three months to a year.

Key Point: For a successful acceptance plan, the parties must specify clearly thc performance and performance specification (i.e. what the software and solution are intended to perform). In addition, the acceptance test document has to outline the case where the software or the system fails to pass the acceptance tests after being repeated several times and the consequences of such failure, as well.

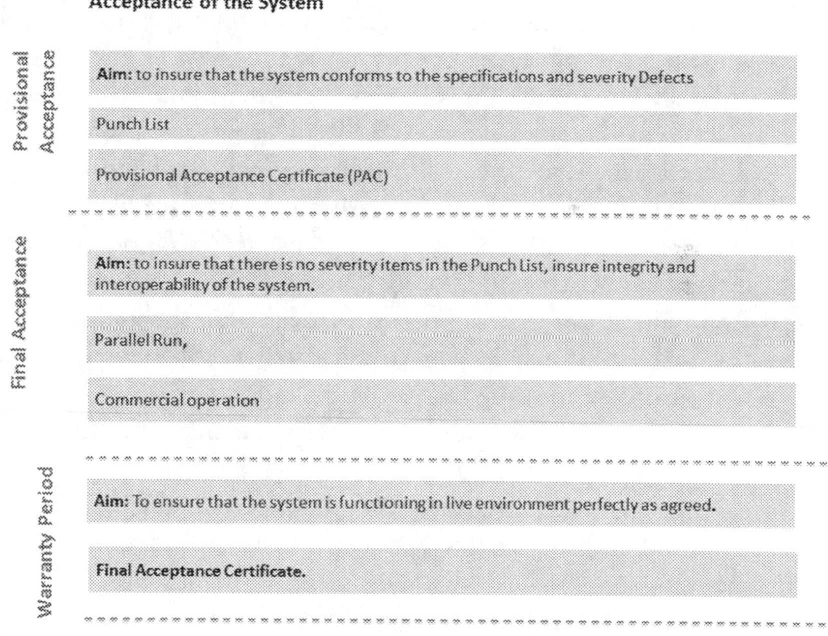

Figure 10: Acceptance of the Turnkey System

Liability

The ground rule stipulated by ME laws (article 157 Egypt, article 272 UAE, article 209 Kuwait) states, "In contracts binding on both parties, if one of the parties does not do what it is obliged to do under the contract, the other party may, after giving a notice to obligator, require that the contract be performed or cancelled. The judge may order the obligator to perform the contract forthwith or may defer (performance) to a specific time, and he may also order that the contract be cancelled and compensation paid in any case if appropriate".

Here we note the following:

1. The law entitles the aggrieved party to either opt for the resumption of the contract and obligating the other party to carry out its obligations (should that be feasible); or to request terminating the contractual relationship (contract revocation); while being eligible to compensate for the damages incurred in both cases. The laws in ME stipulated that should the dispute be presented before a judge, he shall have vast discretionary authority, and shall be entitled to either grant the offending party a grace period and refuse termination; or approve termination (revocation); or adjudicate to compensate the aggrieved party in light of the relevant circumstances.
2. Contractual liability is based on three axes: 1. should one of the contracting parties fail to perform any of its contractual obligations or to delay the same, it shall be deemed as having committed a "contractual fault"; 2. if this fault causes the other party to suffer "loss or damage", the defaulting party commits to affecting compensation to the aggrieved party 3. in case a "causal relation" exists between the fault and the damage incurred.
3. The above is considered a rule of thumb, but we have noted[83] that the parties are entitled to amend this rule, whether by mitigating, restricting, or eliminating it altogether. The parties are also entitled to agree beforehand on the amount of

---

83 See chapter 3, "Modifying the Contractual Liabilty".

compensation due to the aggrieved party in the event the other party fails to fulfil, or delays, its contractual obligations. We witnessed a significant and fundamental difference with respect to this point between the Middle Eastern laws and common-law countries,[84] and in the case of the former, the judge may, at the request of either party, reduce the agreed compensation amount should a party prove the other party has not incurred any damage, or that the loss suffered is not commensurate with the agreed compensation amount. As far as common-law countries, the judge does not enjoy that authority.

4. In some cases, especially if the contractor is in material and serious breach and when the client feels the project is indeed at risk, the contract may allow the client to "step in" and take over its entire activities or a part of it. The legal basis of this type of remedy in the ME legal system can be found in article 381/2 UAE law and article 209/1 Egypt law, which provide that in case the obligation of the contractor is to make a thing or perform a work, and the contractor does not perform such work, the client may seek an order from the judge to step in and perform the work himself if doing so is possible. In the event of urge, the client may perform the work himself without requiring permission from the judge. In both cases, the execution of the work shall be at the expense of the contractor. The same principal was repeated in article 877 UAE law and the 650/1 Egypt law on regulating the provisions of the "contract for work" (Muqawala), stating the contractor must complete the contract in accordance with the terms and conditions of the contract. If it appears that he is carrying out what he has undertaken to do in a defective manner or in a manner that is a breach of the agreed terms and conditions, the employer may require that the contract be immediately terminated if it is impossible to perform the work up to par. However, if it is possible to execute the work of a superior quality, it shall be permissible for the employer to require the contractor to abide by the conditions of the contract and repair the work within a reasonable period. If such period expires without the reparation being performed, the employer may apply to the judge for the cancellation of the

[84] See chapter 3 page, "Liquidated Damages".

contract or to leave himself to engage another contractor to complete the work at the expense of the first contractor.

5. In most cases of turnkey projects, suppliers are responsible for the system design and accordingly must be aware of their responsibilities regarding the whole system. If the system is based on recommendations of the supplier, he will be responsible for ensuring that the hardware, software, and services are adequate and sufficient in order for the system to perform according to the specifications. This corresponds to the fact that if the hardware, software, and services are insufficient, he will be responsible to provide any additional hardware, software, and/ or services in order to cause the system to perform according to specifications.

Limits of Liability

We have explained above the main principals of the contractual liability from the Middle Eastern legal system's perspective. The limitation of liability and remedy provision are very important legal protections should matters take a turn for the worst. We would like to bring some important legal aspects pertaining to this discussion in the Middle Eastern laws to the attention of the contracting parties:

- In accordance with the region's laws, any ambiguity or lack of clarity in contract provisions – including liability – shall be interpreted as being in the favour of the provider, since "doubt shall be interpreted in favour of the contractor (266 UAE and 151/1 Egypt), whereas in common-law jurisdiction, ambiguity is interpreted against the party imposing the text (usually the licensor or the more powerful party during the contract negotiation). Here we encourage all parties to pay special heed while formulating agreements and contracts, so that the wording utilized accurately reflects their intentions.
- Many rules pertaining to liability are "commanding rules", which the parties are not entitled to agree differently otherwise any agreement made in contradiction with the set rules shall be construed as being null and void, and as such parties must

carefully formulate liability provisions and to have them reviewed by the legal counsel.

- Finally, we note that liability insurance[85] may be used during the implementation of IT projects where one of the parties (probably the contractor) insure the potential liability that may arise in case of contract failure.

***Basic guidance*:** Following are guidelines on how to manage risk and exposure pertaining to liability under the Middle East legal system. It will certainly be in the interest of the provider – insofar as software and IT contracts are concerned – to limit the liability arising from his violation of project obligations or delay in fulfilling commitments. In fact, this is a very possible and likely scenario that may be controlled by the provider, as follows:

- Restrict the contract scope as accurately as possible, so that the obligations and commitments of each party are set forth very clearly and concisely. In the event of an error or violation, it is then possible to easily identify the party responsible for the same.
- Specify and limit the warranties and representation provided by the provider and excluding all others. For example, if you are responsible to integrate the system to the network, you should specify that such integration is limited to the current network and does not apply to any future expansion.
- Exclude certain types of legal liability that may arise out of the performance of the agreement by the provider or out of the customer's use of the software or the system. Such as that arising from special, indirect, and consequential damages, loss of revenue, loss of profit, loss of data, loss if saving, incidental damages or other consequential damages etc.
- Limit your liability by setting a ceiling for compensation arising from contract implementation, which is due to the aggrieved party caused by a contractual error. This may come in many forms, such as specifying a certain amount (typically the

85 Liabilty insurance is general insurance industry; where a contract party protect himself by insure the risks of liabilities imposed by lawsuits or otherwise.

maximum limit covered by insurance), or total contract value (if specified), or total contract amount plus a certain percentage (10 or 20 per cent), or licensing fees in case of license contracts, or maintenance fees in the case of maintenance contracts, etc.

- With regard to the liquidated damages clause, it can be limited and calculated based on the part or phase of the project which has been delayed (not the whole system value). The clause should allow the defaulting party some time to remedy the delay. That party should receive a written notice specifying the default and the other party's action. It should be negotiated in parallel with some other clauses such as warranties, limitation of liabilities, IPRs, indemnities and contract price, and payment terms. Make sure which applicable law will be applied, if it is within the common-law legal system ensuring it reflects a genuine estimation and not a penalty. Finally, in the business context, the liquidated damages should not be a way to enrich one party on the account of the other. It should also be directly attributed to the contractor default.

Contract/Project Termination

Chapter 3 has dealt with the termination of the contract from the ME laws' perspective, in which we highlighted that contract can come to its end in different ways.[86] In general, there are two main scenarios:

First, when things go very well and the project is completed successfully. In such case, the contract will be needed normally upon the expiry date and the fulfilment of the parties' obligations.

Second, when contract is terminated during its validity. For instance, when things go the extreme opposite way and the project is collapsed in the middle and the contract has been terminated or rescinded. For the second scenario, there usually exist two cases where a contract is terminated during its validity. *The first case* is due to a legitimate and known reason, called sometimes "termination for cause", the most important of which is having one of the parties breach a core or "material obligation". Here we advise the parties to clearly define what

86 See chapter 3, point titled "End of Contract".

constitutes a "material breach". I refer to the classification of the contract provisions into three groups, as shown in chapter 4. Such grouping will help the parties determine the events of a material breach since the violation of core provisions constitutes material obligations, and breach of which will be deemed material breach. In software and IT projects, for example, this could refer to

a. late delivery, or delay in implementation of the project exceeding an agreed reasonable period
b. software or system fails to pass the acceptance tests in an unsatisfactory manner and after a certain number of trials as per agreed criteria
c. violation of the license terms and conditions by the client
d. not paying the charges when due

There are other events for contract termination, like one of the parties enters into a compulsory or voluntary liquidation or is deemed unable to pay its debts or has an administrative receiver, receiver, liquidator, trustee bankruptcy manager, or administrator appointed over all or some of its undertakings or assets. A substantial change of ownership or management may be considered a reason for termination in some IT contracts, such as a software distribution agreement. Some contracts permit termination should contract implementation be halted for a certain duration (such as ninety days, for instance) due to a force majeure, or should penalties exceed the agreed-upon maximum limit (usually between 10 and 15 per cent).

A contract can be terminated in the event the supplier decides to increase prices (in maintenance contracts, for example). In the above cases, the contract permits one party to notify the other in order to resolve or rectify the violation (where possible), after which the former may terminate the contract unilaterally.

The second case is when the contract avails to the parties (or one of them) the option to terminate the contract "for convenience" (i.e. for no reason), by notifying the other party, which is often an action that is difficult to accept. With software licensing contracts, for instance, the licensee will not accept the licensor terminating the agreement for no reason. In contracts pertaining to turnkey projects, it is difficult for the customer to grant the supplier this power, and vice versa. Therefore, in cases where one party insists on having the right to unilaterally terminate the contract, we advise, especially in the pure IT contracts as specified earlier, to include an indemnity clause whereby the other party to be indemnified absorbs all the losses and damages incurred because of the contract termination without any reason. Moreover, the termination notice in such cases must also be relatively longer (ninety days, for example). However, it is to be noticed that Article 633/1 of the Egyptian Civil Code allows such right (to terminate the contract for convenience) to the employer in Muqawala contracts. In such case, the employer has to compensate the contractor for all of contractor's expenditure, work that has been achieved and for his gain, assuming the work would have been completed.

From a legal perspective, the expiration or termination of contract entails the following outcomes:

- Termination of both parties' commitments, but shall not affect the accrued rights and liabilities of either party up to or including the date of termination. With contract termination, the software license granted to the licensee is also terminated, and the license to use the software will be terminated, unless otherwise agreed.
- Some terms and conditions shall continue in force – by their very nature – such as the confidentiality and non-solicitation clause (refraining from hiring the other party's employees), and some others that will come into force upon the occurrence of termination, such as those related to the exit plan and dispute resolution.
- Some contracts may stipulate certain obligations for both parties, especially upon the supplier, such as assisting the other party upon contract termination. At times, this assistance is outlined in detail in a separate appendix.

***Key Point*:** We would like to reiterate that contract termination in the field of software and IT projects is an unfavourable action that both parties are advised to thoroughly contemplate prior to going forward with. It is something that should only be resorted to when absolutely necessary, simply because of the huge risks associated with it. It entails a substantial loss of time, effort, and investment for both parties. This is not to mention the squandering of further valuable resources if legal action is initiated. It is better for both parties involved to be patient, tolerant, and somewhat forgiving until fulfilling the common goal of project completion.

The contract termination clause is also related to the contract duration, with the exception of where a specific-duration contract (or definite contracts) has expired after running its course, and no agreement has been made between the parties for renewal of the same.

Dispute Resolution

The point raised here is twofold. The first pertains to the applicable law in case a dispute emerges. The second relates to the forum and methods by which a conflict is resolved – either through a common court of law (litigation), or arbitration or alternative dispute resolution (ADR).

a. With regard to the first point, it is important to mention that the contemporary legal systems of the world are generally based on one of three basic systems: civil law, common law and religious law or sometimes combination of these. A huge variation exists between such legal systems due to the variation in the underlying principles and basis on which these legal systems were founded. The legal system of each country is shaped by unique history and many other factors. For that and because of the great implication of this variation on the disputes process and results, it is important to observe which law will apply to the contract in case of disputes. Normally, each party will wish to refer to the law it is familiar with. In such a case, and if each party insists, the parties may choose a neutral ground and opt for a third-party applicable law.
b. In case a dispute or conflict arises regarding the project implementation, contract interpretation, and so forth, both parties should first resort to an amicable resolution by sparing no effort to manage the crisis and attempt to resolve it by means of a direct negotiation. Both parties may also devise a pre-emptive plan with sufficient time intervals, outlining reasonable

efforts for an amicable agreement and an escalation chart – where meetings may begin between the project managers before escalating to upper management, and between upper management before referring to the dispute forum.

c. Both parties could – indeed should – resort to a knowledgeable and independent technical expert (an audit or consultancy firm) in the event a dispute arising between them during the project is of technical nature. The expert could then work with both parties as an expert and not in the capacity of arbitrator, expressing his opinion on the points of dispute. Questions directed to the expert must be clear and concise and his mission must be given a specific duration, with the possibility of considering the verdict a final and binding one pertaining to the point in question.
d. Another method could be a form of mediation, which is a legal forum for alternative dispute resolution (ADR), granting one individual the responsibility of bringing both parties closer in an attempt to reach a middle ground solution. A mediator's mission is different to that of the technical expert in that, the latter produces a strictly technical report without exerting any effort towards dispute resolution, unlike the former one. Other substantial differences exist between mediation and arbitration, one being that the decision reached by the mediator is inherently unbinding, unless otherwise agreed by the parties.
e. Should all efforts end without reaching an amicable resolution, there is no way out except to resort to the official procedures stipulated by the contract, whether through litigation in front of competent court of law or arbitration.
f. In this respect, we recommend arbitration as a forum for resolving the dispute, since most conflicts in the realm of software and IT projects are of a technical nature. In such a case, an arbitrator or arbitration panel may be selected, on the condition the panel be familiar with IT projects.
g. Because of an immense significance of the IPRs, and in an event of a breach or threatened breach of IPRs, and that may cause irreparable damage to the other party, such other party cannot wait for the normal course of dispute resolution but will be therefore entitled to injunctive or any other equitable relief in order to prevent a breach or threatened breach of IPR.

h. Lastly, the issues of venue and applicable law are interlinked. In many ME jurisdictions, the national courts will not apply the substantive laws of a foreign country. In other words, if the parties select Omani (for example) substantive law as a governing law, they must ensure the dispute is heard in Omani courts and not the courts of a foreign jurisdiction. It should be noted that the situation is different with regard to arbitration where parties are free to select any substantive law to be applicable (of course subject to enforceability issue).

For regarding the arbitration clause, we would like to outline the following recommendations:

- The text must be drafted in a comprehensive and lucid manner, since any unnecessary complication or contradiction would deem the clause void and inapplicable, which may result in referring the dispute to a conventional court of law – perhaps contrary to what the parties intended.
- Should the parties wish to refer the dispute to a specialized arbitration authority, it is imperative for the name of that entity to be set out correctly and accurately. Any ambiguity or default may result – at the very least – in hindering arbitration procedures and increasing costs.
- The contract must only stipulate one dispute-resolution solution, whether that be through arbitration or a court of law, instead of combining both methods, which leads to confusion and a greater dispute.
- For the disputes having global nature, we recommend resorting to the DIFC/LCIA arbitration centre. It is one of the best regional arbitration centres (established in February 2008) between the Dubai International Financial Centre (DIFC) and the London Court of International Arbitration (LCIA) (www.difc-lcia.org/).
- At the last, keep in mind that litigation is a risk itself, considering lengthy litigation is an agonizing practice that is often a waste of time, effort, and money. Alternatively, I suggest using the alternative dispute resolution (ADR), which offers a cost-effective, quick, confidential, and business-oriented way to solve disputes.

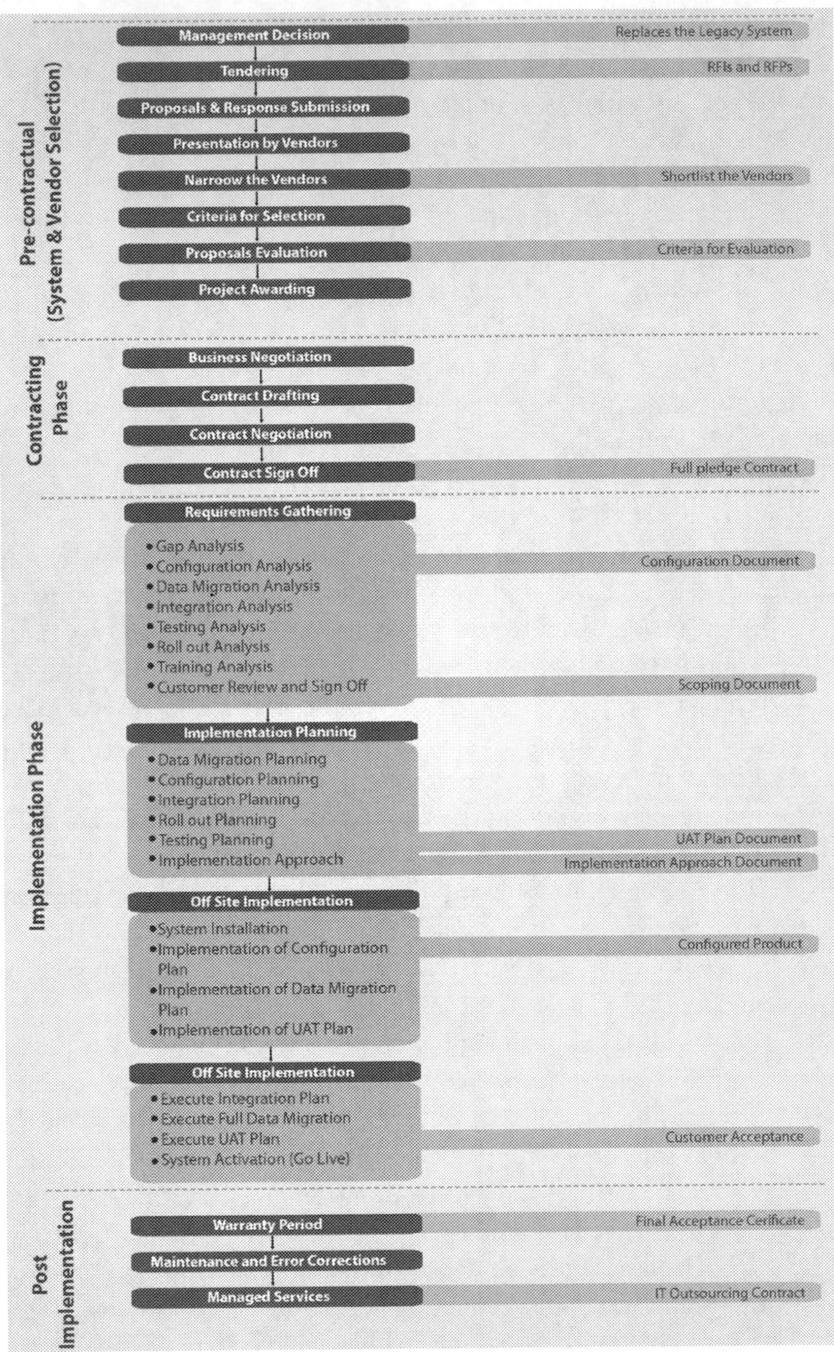

Figure 11: Stages of a turnkey project

Chapter 6
DENOUEMENTS AND KEY INSIGHTS

The New Approach

The rising failure rates of IT projects, together with the increasing risks associated with this industry in general, must not be a source of frustration or disappointment for companies working in this domain, but should perhaps be looked upon as an incentive towards seeking the root of problems encountered and identifying effective tools and remedies, while mitigating risks as best as possible.

The premise of this book is based on the overall theory of contracts, and that of IT and software contracts in particular. This theory is in fact a potent tool lends a hand to the contracting parties in reducing associated risks or avoiding them altogether. This approach is founded on the following four principal elements and assumptions:

1. **Vital Data Gathering** refers to firmly grasping and thoroughly understanding all vital aspects of the project, whether technical, commercial, or legal, such as
   a. purpose of the project
   b. nature of the project
   c. scope of contract (i.e. the products and services constituting the contract)
   d. contracting parties
   e. the party most benefiting from the project
   f. project size and economic costs involved
   g. technology utilized in the project at hand
   h. extent of project complexity insofar as integration with other systems and data migration, etc.
   i. vendors, service providers, primary players, and other players
   j. geographical location witnessing the project implementation
   k. economic and political conditions surrounding project implementation
   l. negotiation position of contracting parties
   m. project duration
   n. integration, data issues, resources, documentations

Any other relevant circumstances, including the tight deadlines and scarce resources, are worthy of being mentioned. We also observe that the aforementioned understanding cannot be achieved without having a cohesive and coherent team comprised of knowledgeable individuals from various specializations and disciplines.

2. **Understanding the Legal Frame:** Next comes a paramount foundation referring to a complete and thorough understanding of the legal milieu surrounding the project starting from the initial contracting steps to their conclusion, through to the implementation phase and thereafter, ending with the possible appearance of the contracting parties before a court of law or arbitration authority. This understanding raises numerous challenges as referred to throughout this book.
   An example regarding such situation is the provisions and process of contracting for turnkey systems, together with resolving the dilemma of the latent defects and lack of conformity to specifications (non-compliance with the project agreed specifications) in IT projects. This includes, among other points, the legal structure of IT and software contracts, as well as all the challenges related to IPRs during and after the implementation of the project, all of which and many others are highly related to the point in hand.
3. **Coherent Contract** refers to a sound and effective formulation of the above-mentioned elements in a clear and comprehensible manner, free of all sorts of cracks, such as those allowing for different interpretations, explanations, or disputes. This is not merely a well-formulated document; rather, it sets forth resolutions and remedies for all situations and possibilities, including the event where the parties fail to complete the project. Hence, the parties are supposed to be capable of predicting events and implementing what has been mutually agreed. Only this way can both parties reach some positive culmination that further leads to the project's success.
4. **Fair and Balanced Contract:** forth assumption lays an emphasis on establishing an impartial and fair balance between the parties including rights, obligations and associated risks. However, this

is to be done in light of a comprehensive understanding of the software industry's customs and traditions, with good faith and honourable dealing. This point in particular pertains to a psychological aspect and presents a focal question, that being the extent to which the parties are capable of relinquishing egocentric interests upon contract signature and practicing a more open and flexible approach with the aim of making the project a success for all. As such, the prime focus would not be so much on achieving a personal victory against the other party, or on obtaining the most concessions at a time when the other party is at its most vulnerable state of desperately attempting to secure a deal at any cost.

Key Insights

Following are summaries of some ideas, tips, and recommendations that may contribute to fulfilling the four aforementioned elements. They may also assist substantially in containing the potential risks accompanying software projects, whether during the negotiation phase or upon formulating and concluding the contractual agreement and beyond, together with all other situations outlined extensively throughout the chapters of this book.

1. The unique nature of the software and IT industry: A meticulous understanding of the nature of the software and IT industry is an ultimate demand for ensuring success. A momentous magnitude of disputes has been occurring between the contracting parties of IT projects, some of which have been brought before courts of law and adjudication authorities. This was a definite consequence of the same lack of understanding, as mentioned. When a crisis occurs, the client often claims the vendor is misleading him into believing in something that does not exist and cannot be achieved, whereas the supplier is of the opinion that the client did indeed acquire what he had been promised, and that any other alleged system functions are nothing but a figment of the client's imagination. Another claim is that the customer is not knowledgeable about his exact needs and as such only seeks to evade payment of the remaining dues.

Key Insight: This leads us to an attempt for identifying common denominators upon which the understanding of the parties may be established, thus the contract can play a pivotal role in this regard, should it prove to be "coherent and fair".

2. The arising legal developments: This point corresponds to the concept of new emerging contractual obligations that IT professionals must be aware of. This means the legal obligations and commitments related to software and IT contracts that have begun to take their rightful place in legal studies and implementations. One example of such is the obligation on the part of vendors (obligation of advice and notification) that necessitates them, being professionals in the field, to inform the client promptly of any important information related to the project, so that the client may choose wisely and correctly. Accordingly, we note the appearance of provisions in numerous contractual agreements obligating a vendor to inform a client who is new to the world of IT for the purpose of increasing efficiency or granting him a competitive advantage.

Moreover, there is another obligation upon the client to cooperate and collaborate in good faith with suppliers to facilitate the completion of the mission at hand. In fact, we are increasingly noting a focus on several commitments and obligations that were once deemed secondary or trivial, such as undertaking to deliver documents, manuals, and user guides, together with training users and rectifying any errors occurring during the warranty period.

Key Insight: Breaching any of these obligations could pave the way for contractual liability, indeed to the collapse of the entire contractual agreement, unbeknownst to the parties thereof. Setting forth the previously mentioned obligations in the contractual agreement constitutes one of the attributes for success, which also emphasizes the urgent need to carefully consider IT and software contracts, being one of the primary keys for success.

3. Apprehend the strength of contract: "autonomy of will" is a significant legal principle that avails extensive leeway for the contracting parties to agree upon various conditions and provisions (so as long it does not contradict with the public order and morality). Indeed, the agreed terms and provisions between the parties assume the force of law, to the extent that the law allows the parties to agree upon issues that may seem logically farfetched, such as for the debtor to bear the consequences of a sudden accident or an event brought about by force majeure (article 217 Egyptian law).

Conversely, it also allows the exemption of the debtor from any liability arising from defaulting on its contractual obligations (except in the case of fraud and blatant error). Even in the event of fraud and blatant error, the parties may agree not to hold the debtor liable should such actions emanate from persons utilized by the debtor in performing its contractual obligations. This applies to the warrantees granted to the client by the vendor regarding the works and products, since most warrantee regulations stipulated by law are not within the domain of public order, and thus the parties may agree on them at their own discretion. A related example would be in the contract to stipulate that the vendor does not guarantee the software being error-free, or that the software has been delivered "as is" without any warranty.

Key Insight: This explicitly shows the notable power and exceptional flexibility bestowed by law upon the contractual agreement regarding regulating matters between the parties, which are in turn required to benefit from these available options in achieving a much-needed balance towards success.

4. Turnkey is a Muqawala contract: Through the pages of this book, this significant and controversial aspect has also been emphasized. As far as the scope of IT and software contracts relating to the sheer quantity of products and services pertaining to IT projects that are associated with the legal nature of such contracts, this matter is important to shed light on. Basically, a contract's legal nature, together with the legal nature of a vendor's commitment, define the overall legal regulations applied to the contractual agreement. But implementing these legal regulations is more challenging than specifying the legal nature of those contracts.

Should we assume, argumentatively, a great portion of these contracts constitutes "contracts for works"? Thus, it becomes tremendously difficult to apply such regulations on the contracts governing and regulating projects possessing a unique nature, which were unknown to the legislator at the time of drafting these provisions. This as well applies to a considerable number of legal issues to which there does not exist any concrete answer, such as liability for latent defects and nonconformity defects. So a contractual agreement is crucial in mitigating controversial issues alongside preventing uncertain outcomes.

Key Insight: The effort exerted in formulating the contract, examining the primary and fundamental aspects of the project, and drafting these in a clear and succinct manner – together with the presence of adequate legal knowledge – is much more desirable than arguing over the legal nature; indeed, it would greatly contribute to avoiding these kinds of risks.

5. Examining latent risks: A diligent and meticulous examination of potential risks encountered by IT projects ahead of time is one of the undeniable measures and actions taken to ensure the success of that project. Regarding this concept, we would like to quote Louis M. Brown, the father of preventive law: "It usually costs less to avoid getting into trouble than to pay for getting out of trouble".

And the same was experienced during the course of chapter 1, whereupon dissecting such risks, we scrupulously observed that these may be viewed from several perspectives. Among the most conspicuous was dividing the same into technical, commercial, and legal risks. Doing so facilitates a thorough examination on the part of three designated teams from each discipline.

Key Insight: A detailed and closer inspection of the risks and uncertain outcomes that may appear at later stages prevents a number of controversies and failures.

6. Scope of contract: We have repeatedly focused on contract subject matter throughout this book and declared it as one of the cornerstones of any agreement. It has been emphasized to an extent that without a subject matter, the contract would be deemed null and void. Why does this aspect hold such a dynamic significance? This question is answered by the following:

i. Contract subject matter constitutes a primary obligation for the parties involved and thus must be a possible undertaking, a specific one (identified), or one that could be identified.
ii. It may be a futuristic endeavour, as is the case of many IT and software agreements, where it is not actually present at the time of contract.

The challenge confronting the parties here is their ability to specify contract subject matter (or scope of work) in a precise manner, for should the extent of ambiguity result in failing to do so, which is not very likely (such as if the intended IT system is based upon a non-exist technology or one that has not been yet finalized), the entire contract could be subject to voidance.

Key Insight: Absence of a clear and concise scope of work, even in the case of a valid contract, paves the way for conflict and could be the grounds for terminating the relationship between the parties altogether.

7. Categories of IT contracts: The area of software and IT is categorized by two main categories of contracts:

i. Pure IT contracts: Being closely associated with the IT and software industry, they pertain to a product, service, or IT project. Such contracts assume special significance, being the mainstay of the IT and software industry.
ii. Contiguous contracts: The contracts belonging to this category are "contiguous" to the above category yet do not constitute pure IT contracts, despite being frequently utilized in IT projects such as confidentiality agreement, teaming agreements and professional services agreements.

Key Insight: Individuals operating in the software and IT field are invited to familiarize themselves with the divisions and utilizations of these sets of contracts, since they are construed as being the basic constituents in the software and IT industry, in addition to playing a vital role in addressing risks.

8. Three levels of provisions were distinguished under the umbrella of categories of IT contracts. From these levels, core provisions incorporate fundamental obligations of the contracting parties, or core pillars upon which the agreement is based, whose presence is vital for achieving the desired outcomes. While acknowledging the importance of all other provisions, these provisions, in particular, are closely associated with software and IT contracts and play a pivotal role in avoiding risks pertaining to software and IT projects, if they are identified and properly utilized. Such provisions assist us in

a. identifying the nature and type of contract,
b. accentuating the material obligations of the contracting parties
c. considering any breach of the same is construed as being a material breach

The other two types of provisions are general and housekeeping provisions, which exist in IT contracts, as well as contracts in other industries. These require focused attention.

Key Insight: Through these levels of provisions, one can understand the nature and other relevant details of the contract in a fathomless manner and then use it to achieve the target.

9. Contract is a significant legal structure: Since the contract is the law of both parties, the following essentials are mandatory:

i. The contract cannot be modified or terminated except as stipulated in the contract or by law, this is a fundamental and primary rule in all laws of the region.
ii. A contract commands a legally binding power, indicating that what both parties agreed to in the contract becomes obligatory, an irrevocable commitment on the part of each unless allowed by the contract itself or by law.

iii. The parties should not underestimate the contract power. This is also why signatories must always be sure to double check contractual contents prior to signature.

All professional in the software and IT industry should be sure that the contract is in a highly significant legal structure. Moreover, it is a remarkable and versatile tool for the decision makers, legal experts, and for the professionals involved in the commercial field. The contract can be effectively used to prevent complications at the outset, and avoid or at least mitigate the effects of risks present in software and IT projects.

Key Insight: The contract holds a powerful legal value for all professionals. All those employed in the area of software and IT (especially sales personnel) must accustom themselves with common commercial practices and customs associated with the software industry, as they hold considerable weight in interpreting the contract should disputes arise.

10. Clarity: Through this concept, we have put hard efforts into emphasizing the influence of a clear and lucid contract. Undoubtedly, clear contract provisions, rights, and commitments contribute to increasing a project's success rate, yet as simple as these words may seem, their implementation is something that demands adequate attention. The term "clarity" asks for a perfect understanding of both parties. Moreover, the language used in the contract must accurately reflect the desire of the parties, their common intentions, and true undertakings.

Perhaps both parties opt to summarize terms or ignore them altogether, thinking they adequately understand one another or comprehend what each means to express. This is a drastic and detrimental mistake, since the weight of the contract is not positioned high at the time of signature, but later gets amplified with a rise of disputes and intricacies. In order to enjoy a healthy contractual agreement, the contract must possess the following characteristics:

(i) retain a legible and understandable language in the contract
(ii) prevent lengthy content, since lengthy contracts are tedious and cumbersome, and clarity is all about precision and accuracy

Key Insight: A clear, precise, and complete contract increases the success rate of a project. Stating each and every point in a simple and clear tone enables both parties to understand each other's wills and intentions.

11. Law for the ambiguity of contract: The law in ME has laid the groundwork for interpreting some ambiguous provisions present in the contractual agreement. The rules and regulations for contract ambiguity interpretation are set for in a logical sense, yet the utilization of the same may lead to outcomes that are unintended by one or both parties. To avoid these situations, a clear and concise contract comes across as a potent tool as it shall be viewed, in the future, by other individuals that were not necessarily part of the original negotiation team. Accordingly, all words and phrases stipulated therein must be clear and concise.

Even though the contractual agreement is considered in its entirety, its individual provisions must be formulated on a standalone basis, while employing a cross reference in connecting between those provisions. It must be understood that any judge shall not be able to read the minds of the contracting parties, while also being unauthorized to redraft the agreement between adversaries.

Key Insight: A comprehensive and clear contract with accuracy, precision, and completeness leads both parties to a long-term healthy relationship. Moreover, any documents not in the possession of either party or not attached to the contract should not be referenced, so as not to create any chaos or confusion.

12. Expression of will: The parties must be aware that any expression of the will (which may come in the form of a proposal, a purchase order, or the like) is considered binding, as long as it has come to the knowledge of the recipient. The withdrawal of or change to the offer must reach the knowledge of the recipient on or before that time (the time the recipient came to know about the offer). This simply means that prior to issuing any purchase order or submitting a commercial proposal, that party must review and make sure all the data and conditions are contained therein, otherwise he might not be able to withdraw or make any changes on the proposal if it reaches the other party after the original offer.

Key Insight: A meticulous review of the expression of will before submitting it is a measure taken to mitigate complications and misunderstandings.

13. Legal liability during the negotiation phase: Be aware of this kind of liability, which may appear during the negotiation phase. With respect to the circumstances, they could lead to the existence of contractual or tort liability. All courts have concurred to the existence of a number of legal commitments imposed on the negotiators that are brought about by the negotiation phase. These all emanate from good faith and goodwill, such as candour, cooperation, advice, diligence, moderation, confidentiality, and respecting conventional practices. On the other hand, the contract that was concluded based on deception, cheating, misleading, misrepresentation, or tricks will be liable to cancellation and be considered null and void (article 185/195 Emirate law).

Key Insight: Goodwill at all stages –specially in negotiation phase- strengthens the relationship of the negotiating parties and prevents both from legal misgivings and fraud.

14. Utilizing the contract template: A party may opt to utilize the contract template or precedent (a previously formulated contract template) to make a coherent and fair agreement, and to lay the legal, commercial, and logical foundations. In any case, compiling the first draft will allow you to formulate the contract from your perspective and hence convey your thoughts, demands, and interests from the outset. You can then proceed to argue your standpoint directly; perhaps your thoughts will even lay the groundwork for discussion at a later stage.

However, it is worthy to mention that a complete reliance on any such form is one of the misunderstood concepts because using a template at a rate of 90, 80, or 50 per cent for your contract may be appropriate for your area of business, or it may not. Remember to label the draft something like "draft for discussion", and to use an abbreviation or number for easier monitoring of amendments. While amending a draft submitted to you by the other party, be sure to highlight any modifications made. Here you may want to utilize the track changes feature in the "tools" dropdown menu in MS Word.

Key Insight: These kinds of forms are still nevertheless useful in initiating negotiations, so long as they reflect the dynamic of the computer industry and trade yet require your valuable input and the special touch of your loyal legal advisor.

15. Letter of intent: We advise all relevant parties not to entirely or ultimately rely on the letter of intent, and to carefully review its contents in order to determine the letter's actual legal value. This is so they do not burden themselves with legal commitments and financial load. Often a letter of intent will be subject to the signing of the full-fledged contract relating to the project; hence, its legal value is indeed questionable.

Key Insight: The contracting parties must meticulously review the letter of intent to prevent themselves from unexpected outcomes of legal and financial burdens.

16. Premature initiation of project activities: This action is strictly prohibited by the experts. Both parties may be tempted to start various project activities under the pretence of speed and time-saving efforts prior to concluding contract negotiations – indeed even before signing. This is a momentous error in judgment as it implies one of the parties has proceeded to invest time and resources in the project without reaching a full and common understanding before signing a definite contract.

Key Insight: Starting any kind of project activity before finalizing the negotiation phase results in catastrophic outcomes. In fact, doing so could place one party under pressure for the remaining part of the negotiation.

17. Use a common language in the contract: This is specifically stipulated for the contract being signed between parties of different languages. Using a common language, such as English, facilitates the process of contract formulation. An Arabic version must also be available should disputes be referred to national ME courts.

Key Insight: If a contract is formulated in multiple languages, only one language must be chosen to be the accepted contract language in case of disputes. Some would suggest, in case each party insists on using its own language as reference, that parties not address this problem, leaving it to lie within the jurisdiction of a judge or arbitrator in the future.

18. Accuracy in drafting financial details: A contract cannot attain thorough clarity unless its values and payment methods are outlined clearly and accurately, this being the primary clause of the contract and a source of controversy. Should payments correspond to the completion of defined works (or milestones), then this should also be explicitly stated. All numbers appearing in the contractual document must be written in both numerals and words for the currency to be specified. Also, remember to state the party bearing tax charges, while being careful to set the exchange rate in the event payment shall be made in a different currency than the one set in the contract.

Key Insight: Ensure the clarity of financial details in the way as recommended above. Both parties will preferably agree on prices related to the support and maintenance phase and state the same clearly and accurately. In case it is likely that other services will be obtained from the provider – during or even after contract duration – that are not included, the rate of which must be agreed upon and explicitly stated.

19. Organization of appendixes: It is not necessary to cram all the agreed-upon terms into the contract. Appendixes may be assigned for technical details, analytical drawings, and other elaborations; however, do not be tempted to overlook the formulation and review of those annexes, as they are considered an integral part of the contract. They also contain detailed terms and conditions that are of vital importance for project implementation, in addition to playing a major role in defining the duties and commitments of the parties. Be sure to pay attention to these appendixes and obtain the approval of relevant specialists on what they outline.

Key Insight: Organizing the contractual document by including appendixes paves the way to a more comprehensive contract. When structured in a refined manner, they enhance the readability and understandability of the contract.

20. Making assumptions: Do not assume anything and place every point up for discussion, negotiation, and clarification. Do not presume the other party knows what you mean, or that an "implied agreement" exists between you regarding a certain term or clause. A sound contract assumes nothing.

Key Insight: The negotiation phase is the core of an IT project; therefore, leaving any point that must be discussed makes room for ambiguities and vagueness. Instead of making assumptions, the contracting parties must come to a meeting table for discussion and clarification.

21. Boilerplate terms: Be attentive to standard clauses that appear in all contracts. These are the ones that usually appear towards the end of the contract and are referred to as boilerplate terms, like applicable law, dispute resolution, notices, confidentiality, and the like. In spite of the importance and efficacy of these clauses in the rights and obligations of the parties, they continue to be overlooked more often than not by the contracting parties. We advise that these clauses not be taken at face value, but that they be questioned and discussed, with their repercussions made clear and firmly understood, for they may equate or even exceed the importance of other clauses once thought more influential.

Key Insight: Get a firm grasp on every detail of the contract. We advise that these clauses (boilerplate terms) not be taken at face value, but that they be questioned and discussed, with their repercussions made clear and firmly understood, for they may equate or even exceed the importance of other clauses once thought more influential.

22. Dispute-resolution mechanism: When large and expensive projects are executed, conflicts will prevail. By devising a clear-cut and thorough dispute-resolution mechanism, these conflicts may be addressed. Hence, a sufficient time must be set aside for attempting to amicably resolve any disputes. With the existence of a probability for setbacks comes the potential rise of tedious and costly disputes that could spill into courts of law or arbitration arenas.

It therefore pays to agree beforehand on a specific mechanism dealing with the aches and pains of legal disputes and thus saving precious time, effort, and money. In the event of a dead end, there must be a pre-set exit strategy, which guarantees the minimum damage and harm from project collapse or contract termination. This should contain, among other things, the assistance that could be extended from the provider to the client to restore things or aid in the appointment of another provider. In dead-end events, parties should consider alternative forms to resolve disputes (ADR) as they are quick and cost-effective.

Key Insight: Both parties can save valuable time and money through a proper agreement on the dispute-resolution mechanism. A well-drafted contract can play a significant role to prevent trouble at the outset. Remember, it costs less to prevent troubles than to get out of them. When controversies happen, parties should act fast to contain disputes at their birth.

23: Special word to vendors: Whatever is mentioned about the balance between the parties in the contractual relationship, whereas neither party should be overshadowed to the other; the fact that has been manifested through the daily practices is that the contractor (or service provider) in IT projects is the main player in such interesting experiments, with the major part of responsibility on his shoulders. The contractor is responsible for the system design, planning, and execution until the final delivery of the system, and probably beyond that in the live operation. Accordingly, he is taxed with a paramount part of legal responsibility.

As per the Middle Eastern legal system, there exists a straightforward legal concept behind this. That is, the legal obligation of the contractor is an obligation to achieve a specific result to the extent that if such a result is not acquired, he is in breach of such an obligation and will automatically be held liable. That is because his responsibility in such a case is assumed, once the result was not achieved.

The contractor finds no way to remove such liability, except to prove that such a breach is an outcome of an "external reason" on which he has no control, such as a force majeure or the default of the other party. If he cannot prove otherwise, he will remain responsible. This is despite the fact that both parties suffer from the risk and exposure in the planning and execution of the IT projects. For that, we believe the contractor holds an extremely risky situation, since he is in a position of taking a great part of responsibility of project failure. Such responsibility can sometimes be disastrous. In brief, the contractor in IT projects falls between two jaws: a) his contractual liability, which is built upon the legal assumptions to achieve a result; and b) the difficulty if not the impossibility of achieving such a result in the real life of the software and IT industry.

Key Insight: We urge vendors, service providers, and suppliers in the field of building and delivering an IT turnkey system to pay utmost attention to what they promise. They must make themselves fully aware of what they have committed to doing. The fact is, while they share the risk with their clients, the major part of heat and liability lies on their shoulders.

24. Duty of good faith: Last but not the least, my greatest piece of advice is related to fair trading. The contracting parties in their dealing should seek justice, honour, good faith, honesty, and integrity whether before, during, or after the project. These are all prudent and positive principles that are vital in all walks of life, including the domain of commerce and trade. In essence, all contracts must be founded upon good faith, fair dealing, and honour, and any court of law will surely reject all interpretations based on ill will, misguidance, and deception. This does not only apply to the phase following contract signing but anything prior to that (negotiation) and after (implementation).

Key Insight: The duty of "good faith" is one of the prime principles present in all laws of the region. It represents the overall framework of the contractual relationship throughout its various phases, the breach of which constitutes a contractual transgression. In order for the parties to act in good faith and duty, they must avoid intentional error, fraudulent behaviour, abusing their rights, and blatant errors.

=====================

Chapter 7

THE ROLE OF THE IN-HOUSE LEGAL COUNSEL

Background: Regarding today's trend, an in-house legal team can and should play a significant role in the commercial aspects of their organization by aligning the legal services with the organization's business needs, and bridge the gap between the theoretical legal topics and the actual business needs. Moreover, they can contribute to the strategic business planning, change and process management, and major commercial opportunities and projects. In my last 20 years, I had some very interesting practice being part of my company's management team. My team and I were always part of the management team offering great contributions, providing high-value support to the company's development and its strategy planning.

Accordingly, and as related to the theme of this book, a legal team can play a significant role in the success of company IT projects. The team can easily be a vocal point, particularly in the pre-contractual phase and the overall contractual process. In-house lawyers should move outside their comfort zone to where they add real value to the business. In particular, in house counsels can play an important role towards the success of IT projects.

How?

You have first to educate yourself about the development of the IT industry in general and update yourself on the rapid changes and new areas of software, such as SaaS (software as a service), Open Source, cyber-security, and data protection. You should also know the big players (vendors) in your specific industry and the related major IT solutions. You should educate yourself the different types of software and background of IT projects and unique features of IT turnkey projects.

This will also assume full knowledge about your organization its business, structure, competitive edge, and policies. This is because implementation of IT projects in some organizations entails more risk than in others. It is subject to the size of the organization, the business complexity, company data integration, current system, and so on and so forth.

You should be aware of distressing phenomena found in the IT industry (as illustrated in this book) – that is, the rate of failure in the IT industry is very high. Sixty per cent of IT projects sadly fail in different ways and to different degrees. Moreover, all projects are unique; no two organizations face the same challenges. Knowing this will convince the team to be extremely cautious.

When an organization decides to replace the legacy system,[87] some fundamental decisions have to be made. An in-house lawyer must be aware of such decisions. Having a new system is not a transaction that happens frequently, but knowing the basics of such a transformation will enable the legal team to effectively participate, especially in the pre-contractual phase, which is fundamental to the project success and will add value to the organization's objectives.

When you participate in an IT project, introduce yourself to the project team, which usually involves senior management; members from sales (who close the deal); the project manager (as a representative of the project team); commercial and procurement; legal and technical leaders; external consultants; and system integrators. Teams must understand each other and know the company's concerns and objectives. They must also keep good communication among the team, talk the same language, and ensure harmony and cooperation.

Become an integral part of the project team at an early stage. It is indeed a wrong practice when management involves the legal team near the end of the transaction. Get closer to the constituents of the project team. Understand their needs, concerns, and caveats. Learn their language and speak it. On the other hand, educate them on some legal principals and concepts that will help them understand the contract basics and structure.

Your value can be brightly demonstrated in the pre-contractual phase, where the fundamental features of the new system are crystallized. Also, some very important documents, such as the "scoping document", are produced and agreed upon during this phase, which resulted from gathering client requirements. This document will be the base of the

87 Legacy system is the old system that needs to be replaced.

"scope of work document", which will be a fundamental part of the contract and will highly influence the project implementation.

It is the role of the in-house legal counsel to wrap up the contract document and make sure the process is clear and correct, that what has been agreed to is well documented before signing the contract and before starting the project. In addition, some crucial legal documents will be signed and entered into at this stage, such as the "team agreement", and a subcontract labelled "confidential and NDS".

Watch what you promise, abide by your company's policies, and finally, get everything in writing.

Ask Non-Legal Questions

Following is a general checklist in question form that should be asked by the legal counsel who is part of the negotiation team, whether to himself or to other team members. The list clearly indicates how the in-house counsel can demonstrate significant value to his organization, how his contributions can affect the project's success, and how the contracts can be a significant tool to alleviate the risks and increase project success rates in the IT world. It also constitutes a type of exercise for mastering the art of contract drafting.

While we are confident you can take care of the complicated legal aspects of the project, do not hesitate to ask non-legal questions. It will help you to greatly understand the project major elements. Use the answers as a reference to your contract, in a way to avoid any potential pitfalls and accordingly increase your participation in the project success:

The Project:

- Are your well-versed in the project?

- Have you seen a "summary of the project"?[88]
- Does the project fall within the scope of the software and IT industry?
- Have you seen the risk identification and risk analysis reports?
- Is there accurate project governance and control?
- Do you believe the project is supported by the organization?
- Is the project "tender-based"? Have you read the tentative terms?
- Are there accurate criteria for selecting the vendor?
- Have the project management team been chosen?
- Has the implementation methodology been figured out?
- Have any agreements been signed with any third-party vendors related to the project (e.g. teaming agreements, NDAs, subcontracts)? Have you seen them?
- Did you take into account the value and the strategic importance of the project?
- Is a negotiation team has been formed?
- Are you (or one of your team) is a member of the negotiation team?
- Are you knowledgeable of the company objectives of the overall project?
- Are you knowledgeable of the other party status and previous history?
- Is the negotiation team aware of the basic legal environment and contract law?

The Contract Document

- Are there any legal other documents signed between parties related to the project?
- If yes, is any of these documents affect your contract?
- Is your contract affected by any of these documents?
- Is any of these documents MOU?
- Is it legally binding?

88 "Summary of the project" is a brief description of the proposed system and other related aspects of the project. The summary should be in a simple language that can be understood by the entire project team member, in particular the non-technical team members.

- Can it be used as a concrete legal basis to start the project?
- If not, has the company started the project implementation?[89]
- If yes, on what legal basis?
- Does the contract fall within the "pure IT contract" purview?
- Do you have pre-existed standard form?
- Can you make it base for discussion?
- Did you choose the right form?
- Are the parties' details correct and complete?
- Did you identify who is licensing the system (or the software)?
- Did you identified the core provisions (terms fundamental to the operation of the transaction)?
- Did you make sure that the contract contain the other usual standard terms?
- Did you identify to whom the software will be licensed and who may have the right to use it?
- Have you agreed on the language to be used for contract formulation?
- Have appendixes been compiled for technical aspects of the project?
- Have these been reviewed and confirmed by experts?
- Is the contract being used to document and "codify" every element of the project?
- Have all the parties to the transaction the necessary authority to enter into the agreement?
- Overall, do you believe the contract as a tool for project success is coherent and balanced?

The System/Software

- Is the new system a Greenfield or Brownfield?[90]

89 I have indeed seen companies start the implementation based on verbal discussion.

90 Greenfield and Brownfield are an IT industry terms describe the implementation of the system whether it is new system i.e. no old system to be replaced (Greenfield), or replacement to an old (legacy) system (Brownfield).Brownfield system usually associated with a lot of troubles related to integration and data migration.

- Is there a legacy system?[91] Do you know about it?
- Is the new system "off the shelf", "rented", or developed from scratch?
- Are the products and technology that will the base of the system available?
- Will there be any integration activities and data migration?
- Is there a comprehensive description of the system?
- Are the system specifications well defined?
- Is the specifications properly reviewed, agreed and signed off by upper management?
- Does the type of license (to use the system) responding to the nature of the system?
- How many acceptance tests will the system be subjected to?
- Was the acceptance plane/criteria well developed, agreed upon, and signed by both parties?
- What are the procedures if the system (or any part of it) fails to pass any acceptance tests?
- When will the system (or any part of it) be deemed "accepted"?
- Are any escrow arrangements needed?
- What are the indemnity arrangements and remedies against claims that the system (or the software) infringes third-party rights?

Teams and Resources

- Is there a negotiation and project team[92] already in place?
- Do you think the implementation team is sufficient and skilled enough? Is the implementation team in place?
- Is there a backup of resources in case a member of the team leaves?
- Did you introduce yourself to the project team?

---

91 Legacy system means the old system that will be replaced.

92 The project team is different from the implementation team. The responsibility of the project team starts from the emerging emerge of the idea of having a new system until signing the contract. The responsibility of the implementation team starts with the project kickoff.

- Overall, do you think the organization is ready to start the project?
- Are the resources devoted exclusively to the project?

Scope and Parties Commitments

- Have you seen the "scope of the project" document?
- Is it accurate and detailed? Was this confirmed by any concerned staff?
- Is the projcct within the long implementation period, and high risk?
- Are the commitments expected by the parties explicit?
- Have the products, services, and deliverables been listed accurately?
- What is the vendor obligated to deliver under the terms of the agreement?
- Is the responsibility of each party accurately defined as to who is responsible for what? Particularly system design, integration, interoperability, data migration, and hardware capacity needed to run the system?
- Have you noticed any ambiguity regarding any of the parties' obligations?
- Is there any possibility for additional service? Did the parties agree on the scope and prices for additional services?
- Did the contract provide for system support, especially after system activation?
- Did the contract articulate the scope, coverage, and duration of the system warranty, including the remedies or penalties for breach of warranty?
- Did the contract articulate the remedies in case of non-performance of either party?
- Has any issue been suspended (did not agreed and documented in the contract) until after contract signature?

Term and Schedule

- Have the contract terms been defined?
- Is the implementation period realistic?
- Are the implementation phases lucidly defined?
- Is the implementation methodology properly defined and documented?
- Is there a mechanism in case the term has to be extended?
- Does the contract outline consequences for delay or non-performance?
- Does the contract provide for an exit plan in case of project failure?

Amount and Payment

- What is the value of the transaction?
- It is relatively within the high value transaction, and then high risk?
- Are the financial aspects of the project documented in a clear and concise manner?
- Is the contract value in dollar amount (or any other currency) clear and definite?
- Does the contract separately indicate and document the price for any extra services and expenses?
- Has the project budget been agreed upon and allocated?
- Is there a guarantee about the financial status and solvency of the other party?
- Do the payment terms link to deliverables or a specific milestone?

Bibliography

- Clarence H. Riddly, Peter C. Quittmeyer, John Matuszeski, Computer Software Agreements, Forms and Commentary, Warren Gorham Lamont, 1992.
- Chris Edward, Nigel Savage, and Ian Walding, Information Technology & the Law, (1990) 2nd Edition.
- Chris Turner, Contract Law, Key Facts, Hodder&Stoughton, 2005.
- David Salt, Laura Warren, and Alex Hall from Clyde & Co Middle East. "A guide to liquidated and ascertained damages for the Qatar construction scoter". Article by: Justine Reeves and Patrick Murphy from Clyde & Co, Dubai office. "English Contract Law"
- Deltev J. Hoch, Cyriac R. Roeding, Gert purkert and Sandro K. Lindner., "Secrets of Software Success: Management Insights from 100 Software Firms around the World", Harvard Business School Press, 1999.
- Dian Rowland, Uta Kohl and Andrew Charleswoth. Information Technology Law, Fourtth Eddition, Routledge, Taylor & Frncis Group, 2011.
- Harry Beckwith (1997), Selling the Invisible, New York: Warner Books.
- Ian J Lloyd Information Technology Law, Forth Edition, (2011), England: Oxford University Press.
- Phil Simon. Why New Systems Fail, course Technology PTR, Centage Learning 2010

- Paul Rylance, Legal Writing and Drafting, Blackstone Press Limited.
- Raymond T. Nimmer, the Law of Computer Technology, Third Edition, West Group, 1979.
- Richard Raysman and Peter Brown, Computer Law: Drafting and Negotiating Forms and Agreements, 2004, Law Journal seminars-press
- Robert Bond, Software Contracts: Law, Practice and Precedents (fourth edition), Special Report, Tottel, 2010.
- Saad Al-Barrak, "Success and Failure of Information Systems: A Supplier's Perspective", The London School of Management (Royal Holloway), January 2001.
- In addition to a great number of books, articles and references in Arabic language.